Neutral Color Schemes

Neutral
Color Schemes

Neutral Palettes and Dramatic
Accents for Inspirational Interiors

Alice Buckley

A FIREFLY BOOK

A FIREFLY BOOK

First published by Firefly Books Ltd. 2008

Copyright © 2008 Quarto Inc.

Library and Archives Canada Cataloguing in Publication

Buckley, Alice
    Neutral color schemes: neutral palettes and dramatic accents for inspirational interiors / Alice Buckley.
Includes index.
ISBN-13: 978-1-55407-401-3
ISBN-10: 1-55407-401-0
1. Color in interior decoration. 2. Color guides.
I. Title.
NK2115.5.C6B83 2008   747'.94   C2008-900514-7

Publisher Cataloging-in-Publication Data (U.S.)

Buckley, Alice.
    Neutral color schemes: neutral palettes and dramatic accents for inspirational interiors / Alice Buckley.
[256] p. : col. ill., photos. ; cm.
Includes index.
ISBN-13: 978-1-55407-401-3
ISBN-10: 1-55407-401-0

Summary: Features schemes of neutral palettes, showing different color combinations which can evoke a range of moods and atmospheres. Organized by color groups, handbook presents fail-safe color schemes to create tranquil bedrooms, spacious living areas, and light and airy kitchens.
1. Color in interior decoration. I. Title.
747.94 dc22   NK2115.5.C6.B835 2008

Published in the United States by
Firefly Books (U.S.) Inc.
PO Box 1338, Ellicott Station
Buffalo, New York 14205

Published in Canada by
Firefly Books Ltd.
66 Leek Crescent
Richmond Hill, Ontario L4B 1H1

QUAR.NSB

Conceived, designed and produced by
Quarto Inc.
The Old Brewery
6 Blundell Street
London N7 9BH

Project editor: Emma Poulter
Copy editor: Claire Waite Brown
Art director: Caroline Guest
Designer: James Lawrence
Proofreader: Ruth Patrick
Picture researcher: Sarah Bell
Indexer: Diana LeCore

Creative director: Moira Clinch
Publisher: Paul Carslake

Color separation by Modern Age Repro House Ltd., Hong Kong
Printed in China by Midas Printing International Ltd.

Contents

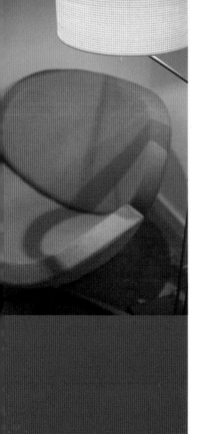

THE COLOR PALETTE DIRECTORY

About this book

This book features 200 neutral color schemes to inspire home decorators and interior designers. With useful information about the colors and the mood evoked by each, this is an invaluable resource that will help you to select a scheme and then create the perfect room, whether it be a warm and relaxing living room, a sexy, sumptuous bedroom or a light and airy kitchen.

The book begins with an introduction to neutrals—our perception of them, how they have been used throughout history, their influence and how they figure in the modern world. Once a brief overview has been established, the basic principles of color theory are explained to provide you with a sound foundation from which to build upon.

While it is useful to have some understanding of color principles, it is ultimately the relationship between these colors and the mood created by them that is important when implementing any interior scheme. The following pages discuss the different moods evoked by certain color groups and how and where to get inspiration, before identifying the factors that influence our color choices and why.

Neutrals are one of the easiest groups of colors to work with. They are extremely versatile and can be layered, mixed and matched. The final chapter, the color palette directory, examines the huge array of neutral colors and combinations available, with ideas on all aspects of home decoration and furnishing, to help you create the perfect neutral interior.

Using the color palettes

1 – Color-coded bullets correspond to the color chapter that you're in.

2 – Mood-enhancing words to help you imagine the feeling each scheme will evoke.

3 – The inspiration behind the scheme's color choices.

4 – The theory behind the interior-design style. Find ideas and inspiration on materials and finishes, flooring, furniture, patterns and accessories.

5 – The main color in the room, usually to be used on the walls, although sometimes furniture or flooring may be the main focus.

Take this book into your local DIY store and ask them to match a test pot to this color. Paint a square of color on your chosen area and let it dry, as paint always changes color when it dries. Live with the color for a day or two before committing to a whole room.

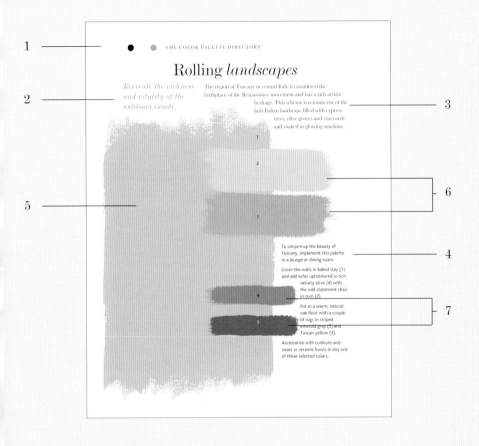

1

2

3

THE COLOR PALETTE DIRECTORY

Rolling *landscapes*

Recreate the richness and vitality of the outdoors inside.

The region of Tuscany in central Italy is considered the birthplace of the Renaissance movement and has a rich artistic heritage. This scheme is reminiscent of the lush Italian landscape filled with cypress trees, olive groves and vineyards and soaked in glowing sunshine.

6

5

To conjure up the beauty of Tuscany, implement this palette in a lounge or dining room.

Cover the walls in baked clay (1) and add sofas upholstered in rich, velvety olive (4) with the odd statement chair in corn (2).

4

Put in a warm, natural oak floor with a couple of rugs in striped emerald gray (5) and Tuscan yellow (3).

7

Accessorize with cushions and vases or ceramic bowls in any one of these selected colors.

6 – Accent colors, which can be used for an adjacent wall, for woodwork or to match to upholstery fabrics. The colors may be darker or lighter tones of the main shade, shades to balance a room or complementary colors that create a contrast in your chosen interior.

7 – Each scheme also features two further highlight accent colors. These can take the form of a sharp injection of color, such as a red vase in a very neutral pale blue interior, or the final balancing tone in a range of harmonious colors, such as a rich, chocolate brown in a room of soft, creamy toffee tones.

Although only used in small quantities, the highlight colors are often the most important shades of all, since they complete the design.

Introduction

"Home" is one of our most evocative words. It conjures up an image of warmth and shelter, of family and friends, a place of inspiration, sanctuary and peace. With so much that's important represented by this one place, it's no wonder that we're passionate about our homes and work to make them ever-more comfortable and welcoming.

Today's homes fulfill many functions beyond shelter and nurturing. We decorate our homes in ways that not only enable them to fulfill these needs but also to reveal our personalities, our aspirations, the very essence of ourselves and how we want others to see us. There are many ways of doing this. Among them are light and color, two qualities that surround us in our natural environment, which can dramatically influence and alter our living space. With these two magic wands we can dictate the energy of a space, its mood and comfort level. If we use them well, light and color can help us create a home that supplies the emotional and functional needs we look for in our homes and make them truly our own.

Understanding neutrals

Among the many color palettes at our disposal, neutrals are probably the least understood. These colors are often dismissed as bland and nondescript, thought of as suitable only for hotels or homes about to go on the market, but neutrals have moved beyond those colors not found on the color wheel, such as white, black, gray, brown and tan. The latest neutrals are sophisticated hints at gentle color, and it's this subtlety that makes neutrals so exciting, versatile and effective.

Recent years have seen an emergence of a new crop of colored neutrals. As we all strive for serenity

within our homes, merging hints of colors that are muted and moody create new, fresh schemes for our homes. Deep and dark hues such as khaki, olive and steely gray through to the lighter pink beiges of taupe and mink all form part of the modern neutral palette. With a huge range of color ideas, this book aims to help you make the most of new neutrals in your interior scheme and to achieve the mood or feeling you hope for in each room of your home.

USING TEXTURE
A skillfully constructed neutral interior crammed with texture and reflective pieces creates a sophisticated living space. Textured floor coverings and soft furnishings are pleasing to the eye and the touch, while the ceramics, Perspex table and feature mirror reflect and maximize the natural light.

Neutrals through history

Cast away your preconceptions. Neutral isn't a euphemism for bland. The many tones and hues that fall into this category are an invitation to layering, contrast and texture. With or without an accent color, neutrals can be as exciting as any scheme plucked from the color wheel, yet they bring peace and serenity to our interiors and to our increasingly stressful lifestyles.

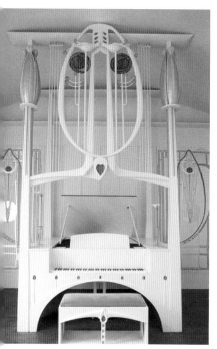

ORNATE ART NOUVEAU
The natural, flowing lines here are complemented by the glowing simplicity of rich cream studded with a jewel red accent. A complex palette of colors would make the scheme over busy and confusing.

Choosing neutrals doesn't necessarily mean choosing contemporary. Many of the divergent decorative styles that evolved during the 20th century look sensational with neutral schemes. At the end of the Victorian age, Art Nouveau, whose sensuous, curvy lines are associated with muted, natural tones, was also the era of the architect and designer Charles Rennie Mackintosh, whose all white and black and white interiors still look cutting-edge today. The glamour and excitement of Modernism, which took off in the 1920s, was an extraordinary display of innovative design—think black leather and chrome furniture set in sensational schemes of silver, black and white, and accessorized with fabulous animal prints.

Changing styles

Elegant Art Deco, with its stylized images and geometric shapes, was also at the height of its popularity during the 1920s and 1930s. It employed the same neutral schemes as modernism, as well as introducing elegant ivory and oyster alongside mother-of-pearl, polished and inlaid wood, black lacquer, stainless steel and startling black and white checkerboard linoleum floors. Shiny fabrics added texture and luxury to schemes that were monochrome yet mesmerizing. In Scandinavia, the

CLASSICAL ARCHITECTURE
Striking architectural features in neutral stone,
marble and iron need little embellishment, though
the mood of the room can be dictated by different
styles of floral decoration.

ACCENTUATING ACCENTS
Never underestimate the importance of accent colors. Part of the beauty of a neutral color scheme such as the one above is that flashes of contrasting or bold colors can be included to bring a sense of fun into an otherwise utilitarian room.

1930s saw the emergence of a cool, pared-down, functional style with the accent on blond wood, natural materials, functional furniture and neutral tones from ecru to bright white with color accents. Many of the designers prominent in this movement, including Arne Jacobsen and Alvar Aalto, are just as popular today. And, of course, Ikea promotes its own ubiquitous version of the look in its own style.

The postwar 1950s was the age of kitsch and bright Formica, yet ice-cream pastels, chrome appliances and design classics from the furniture studio of husband-and-wife team Charles and Ray Eames are perfect accessories for neutral schemes, as is the black and white op art of the flower-filled, color-crazed 1960s.

Neutrals today

While neutrals can be adapted to most interior schemes, that's not the only reason for their current popularity. The wheel of fashion turns inexorably, and it was inevitable that the bright colors and busy schemes so popular in interiors of the 1980s and early 1990s would give way to visually less demanding interiors. In today's modern age, neutrals in the home help to bring peace and calm into our lives. Light and space, both of which can be enhanced and maximized by the use of neutrals, are vital factors for our well-being, and their importance in our hectic lives should never be underestimated.

CREATING CONTRAST
The glass lamp, with its delicate lilac-gray shade, brings a surprising stab of femininity to the dark forest green of this rather masculine bedroom. The texture of the cushions and bedspread add interest to the neutral scheme.

Color theory

A world without color is unthinkable. From the glory of a landscape or the stunning plumage of a bird, to the wonder of a rainbow, a breathtaking flower or the food on our plates, color enhances our lives. Understanding basic color principles will turn your neutral scheme into a sensational interior.

Hering's color wheel

Building upon Issac Newton's color spectrum, the seven colors of the rainbow, and Thomas Young's discovery of the three primary colors that make up light—red, green and blue—Ewald Hering developed his own version of the color wheel, giving yellow as the fourth "primary" color. Yellow, he argued, ought to be a primary color because it is seen by the eye as an independent color, along with red, green and blue. He also included black and white as basic visual primary colors. Hering described his order of colors as "the natural system of color sensations." Today, this system forms the basis of the Natural Color System (NCS), which is used universally as a color-matching tool.

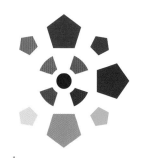

HERING'S WHEEL
The four-color primary wheel was developed in 1878 by German physiologist Ewald Hering. The inner range of brown neutral colors has been added, within each of the 4 quadrants. These browns are created by mixing the four primaries in varying proportions.

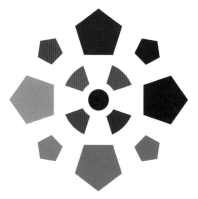

ADDING WHITE
Using the Hering color wheel as a basis, this wheel shows that by adding white, the resulting paler colors form a range of subtle tinted whites.

ADDING BLACK
By adding black, a range of darker neutral shades is achieved. With both these wheels, the same concepts of harmonious and complementary colors apply.

Harmonious colors

When the four pure "primary" colors of red, blue, green and yellow are mixed with their neighbors on the wheel, the secondary colors of purple, turquoise, orange and lime are produced. As you move around the wheel you can immediately see the harmonies between the colors adjacent to each other. The same principles apply with neutrals—a soft buttermilk yellow will always work well with a burnt orange.

Complementary colors

These are the opposing colors on the wheel that vibrate against each other, or clash. Used cleverly in a scheme, these can be striking. Interestingly when two opposite complementary colors are mixed they make a neutral gray—this can be seen in the shadows cast from one color onto its complement. The principle can be used in home decoration; if you are using two complements for paint work, try mixing them to make a third neutral color, by definition it will link well into the two main colors.

Tonal colors

Choosing just one color but using it in varying tones is a tonal or monochromatic scheme, and one that is very successful with neutrals. The addition of texture and pattern can help to bring tonal schemes to life but, remember, sticking to one single tone throughout does not constitute a neutral scheme and signs certain death for any interior.

Neutral colors

A neutral color is one without any bias, and is difficult to achieve (and not necessarily desirable) when mixing paint or pigments. Even a true neutral gray when painted in a room, will take on the colors around it. Neutral colors are generally a mix of two to four primary colors that create a variety of grays and browns with the variation of white or black being added to make them into a tint or a shade.

COMPLEMENTARY SCHEMES
The daring scheme of complementary colors above works well thanks to neutral background shades, while the green mosaic of the bathroom below is enlivened by towels, which serve as color accessories that can be changed to alter the mood of the room. Using a harmonious shade alongside the green, such as turquoise, would create an entirely different ambience.

Color and mood

While our homes represent a place of sanctuary and contentment, each room fulfills a different function. The decorative scheme chosen for each should enhance its ability to fulfill that role, creating the perfect mood or atmosphere. Color and light (both natural and artificial) are used to create the required ambience: an entrance hall, for instance, should be welcoming, a bedroom intimate and calm, while a dining room might project a mood of late-night sophistication.

Different color groups create different moods and emotions. Neutrals, however, are just as able to determine the mood of a room, particularly when used with texture and an accent color. For instance, if sunflower yellow is perfect for an entrance hall, a cheery butter beige in a neutral scheme will produce the same welcoming mood, while red-toned neutrals will create a stunning ambience in a dining room. The mood enhancing properties of colors are just as accessible in a thoughtful neutral scheme.

Mood and function

Does it make you smile, shiver or sigh with contentment? It's well known that certain color groups inspire particular moods and lend themselves to being used in particular rooms. While the amount of color used or the depth of the tone may alter the impact, the general principle remains, even in a neutral scheme in which the tone will be subdued or the color used purely as an accent.

A HARMONIOUS SCHEME
Cheerful yet calm, the harmonious greens, yellows and creams of this kitchen work beautifully to create an easy and attractive scheme.

Pinks: Feminine, frothy, fun and happy. A favorite for girls' bedrooms, pinks are also great in drawing and sitting rooms. For neutrals, use candy pink tones or the palest apple blossom.

Reds: Passionate, racy, warm and comforting. Red is the color of life, perfect for reception rooms and dining rooms. For neutrals, make it dark and rich, with the deepest tones of ripe plum or burgundy.

Oranges: Stimulating, fun and warm. Orange is a contradiction, depending on both the shade and its use. Team it with yellow tones to join the wide-awake club or with soft ochers and blues for a Mediterranean dream. For neutrals, stick to burnt oranges and muted tones.

Yellows: Happy, sunny and mellow. Yellow offers a cheery welcome. Not recommended for bedrooms. For neutral variations of this shade, try butter beiges and lemon creams.

Greens: Natural, easy and peaceful. Nature's favorite color works just about anywhere. In a neutral scheme, implement a deep sage or olive green or a grayed basil green.

Blues: Cool, calm, clear and relaxing. The color of sky and water, blue needs good light to look its best. Think pale blues for bathrooms and bedrooms and deeper, grayish tones for dining rooms.

Violets: Pretty, powerful and regal. Use violets with care. Paler shades work in most situations, but save deep, rich violets for sexy bedrooms.

Browns: Rich, warm, earthy colors. Think of the inspirational Italian pigments of sienna, umber, ocher or terra-cotta, and use with the grays and rusty iron colors of natural slate tiles.

Grays: In its purest form, gray is the nearest to the ultimate neutral, as it contains no color, and so acts as a good foil for other brighter colors. Choose from neutral pale dove gray to rich dark charcoal gray, or a gray with a hint of color, such as a velvety mouse gray or a cool Smokey Mountain gray.

COMBINING BRIGHTS AND LIGHTS
The bold reds and pinks of this scheme are neutralized somewhat by the presence of white, resulting in a more balanced room.

Get inspired

The world around us is buzzing with inspiration for neutral schemes. Whether you're in the city, by the sea or in the country, whatever the season and weather and be it natural wonders or man-made works, take a moment to look objectively at anything and everything that catches your eye. Look at the subtle colors of tree bark, from silver birch to dappled limes, the moody grays and pinks of storm clouds, oyster shells with a wedge of bright lemon, a cityscape reflected in a river and the myriad shades in a chunk of stone or a handful of pebbles.

For another perspective, look at these same color themes through the eyes of the masters. How have they been used and interpreted by artists through the ages, by Vermeer, Picasso, Miro, Nash? What is it about one store window, fashion plate or advertisement that draws you while another leaves you cold? You don't have to be an artist yourself to find a palette that pleases you and creates the mood you hope to reproduce in your home.

Using scrapbooks

It's never too soon to start gathering ideas and pasting them into a scrapbook. Packaging, magazine pages featuring anything from fashion and interiors to food and flowers, posters, paint cards, flyers, postcards, birthday cards, holiday snaps, even a photograph of the amazing mix of colors in the coat of a leopard or your pet dog. If you like it, paste it in. Stills from favorite television programs and films are fertile ground. Period dramas, expertly researched and true to their era, are rich with inspiration, but so is contemporary film with lavish locations dressed by the world's best stylists. Model your scheme on *The Godfather's* Sicilian villa or a seascape from *Message in a Bottle*. As your book fills,

GENERATING IDEAS
Little bits of what you like will fill your head with ideas and help you to bring together the perfect scheme. These ideas point toward a mix of rich, warm, earthy neutrals balanced with pattern, a little shine and perhaps a splash of accent color.

Warm yellows and
greens—natural—
what was the film?

Tunisia family vacation
—July 2006.
Amazing architecture
Vivid colors

you'll see a theme developing. Viewing the world with interested eyes will make every trip, however mundane, a journey of discovery.

Mood boards

Once you know what you like, create a mood board. A tool used by designers, a mood board is the distillation of your chosen colors, textures and fabrics. If your scheme has to include something that you won't be changing, such as a carpet or a stone fireplace, include it on the board. If you're building a scheme from scratch, begin compiling the board around your main color. Or you may want to base the scheme around an inspirational starting point, such as a favorite rug or painting, and pick your colors from that piece. Include paint swatches and fabric samples: the mood board isn't just about color but also pattern and texture.

To give as true a representation as possible, place the carpet swatch or wood/tile sample at the bottom of the board, soft furnishing swatches in the center, curtain swatches at the side and paint swatches as appropriate. If your accent color is going to cover a whole wall, it should feature prominently on the mood board. If it will be no more than a pair of cushions, make it proportionately smaller. Anything that disrupts the harmony of the scheme should be removed, no matter how much you like it—you can always use it in another room.

SECONDARY SOURCES
The great artists understood color, so don't be afraid to steal themes, ideas and inspiration from their work to incorporate into your own schemes. These rich reds, golds and browns balanced by palest pink, fawn and cream will create a warm, restful scheme perfect for a sitting room or bedroom.

I love this picture by Vermeer—rich colors. Could it work in my house?

Cushions at mom's!

I remember the trees on the lake in the fall —those golden browns, so beautiful—study color?

Choosing your color scheme

As your neutral scheme takes form there are several influential factors to be considered before you reach for the paintbrush or order your fabric. Mood, function, light and flow must all play a part in your decisions if your scheme is to be a success.

PERFECT HARMONY
Dark wood furniture loses definition in a dark room, but these wonderful chocolate shades are brought to life by creamy walls, while the tall windows, cleverly curtained with pale fabric and blinds, flood the room with flattering natural light that accentuates each shade of fabric and piece of furniture.

The importance of light

Light is the giver of life, not just for the world in general, but also for your scheme and the mood it creates. Get it wrong and your interior will look dull and flat. Get it right and your scheme will glow with balance and harmony. Abundant natural light is on the wish list of every home owner, and, as one of the most influential factors in the success or failure of your interior, it's worth maximizing available natural light with gauzy fabrics, glass, mirrors and light-reflecting colors. In this respect, neutrals are no different than primary colors: lighter shades reflect light and darker ones absorb it.

Natural light: Natural light shows neutrals at their best, but all schemes will be affected by the time of day, the sun's aspect and the quality of the light as the seasons change. If possible, use south-facing rooms during the day so that you can make the most of available light, and perhaps make a north-facing room the dining room, which will be used mostly at night. Warming shades, often used in dining rooms, will also go some way to making up for the colder light of a north-facing aspect.

Artificial light forms: Artificial light can be unkind to color, so it needs to be used thoughtfully. There are three main lighting styles to choose from: task, ambient and mood. Task lighting is strong and direct and used for reading, cooking or other work. Ambient supplies general illumination, but avoid overhead lighting—the ubiquitous pendant hanging from the center of the ceiling is harsh and unflattering and makes colors look flat. (Chandeliers, which throw sensational, diffused light, are excluded from this rule.)

Lamps and wall lighting are kinder and more versatile. You can also light for mood, creating atmosphere, usually intimate and romantic, which is ideal for bedrooms and dining rooms. Fluorescent light is tricky. If you don't really need it give it a miss, even in kitchens.

Importantly, all artificial light alters color. To make sure your color choices work, test them by painting a paper or plasterboard sample (do not paint directly onto the walls) and placing it in various positions in the room, in various lights, before committing yourself.

Flow

To aid flow throughout the house, one idea is to choose a main color and use it in each room as the basis for individual schemes, possibly on the walls but alternatively on the floor or the baseboards.

MODERN DESIGN
Contemporary open-plan homes, which often have mainly white or all white interiors (as shown above and below), are usually designed with a generous use of glass to supply masses of natural light. The double height of the living area also adds to the abundance of light and the feeling of space.

If you choose a tonal scheme, using several shades of one main color, use the lightest shade on the ceiling, the middle shade on the walls and the darkest shade on the lower half of the wall, if you have a chair rail, or on the floor where appropriate. Also consider the type of paint you will be using: at its simplest, the various grades of gloss will reflect light and therefore look lighter than matte.

Texture and pattern

Texture, another important factor in a neutral scheme, not only adds visual and tactile interest but also contributes to the overall mood of a room. One of the joys of a neutral scheme is the fun you can have with texture, from woven natural fibers on the floor and faux fur throws on the sofa or bed to piles of cushions in appliqué, pleated silk, fluffy wool or studded with decorative buttons.

OLD MEETS NEW
The restful sage green of the tongue and groove balanced with cream creates a traditional neutral scheme in this bathroom, though modern fixtures give it a pleasing contemporary edge.

COOLING COLORS
Reminiscent of New England or Scandinavia,
this kitchen's magical, delicate combination
of shades of gray, green and white speak of
the cool light of the northern hemisphere.
The room's obvious functionality makes it
welcoming and pleasant to be in.

Textured components will be more noticeable in a neutral scheme, than any other, so be sure to choose things that you truly like.

Pattern also comes into its own in a neutral scheme. If you choose to have just one pattern in a room's scheme you can afford to go large, perhaps papering one wall with a fabulous bold pattern, possibly in an eye-catching feature color. Shiny materials, such as chrome, steel, black lacquer and marble, also introduce excitement and interest into the calm of a neutral scheme.

Color considerations

Planning one neutral room in a home otherwise filled with color is perfectly possible, so long as the adjacent rooms, visible when the doors are open, don't start a screaming match. A scarlet dining room, for instance, will sit comfortably next to a neutral sitting room if a red-toned neutral or a red accent is part of the scheme, even if only a small part. The same floor treatment running throughout will also unify rooms. Colors in adjacent rooms must always be taken into account.

If you're decorating your home in order to sell it, keep your scheme simple. Sometimes a striking, off-the-wall interior will sell a house, but it's more likely to limit your pool of potential purchasers, whereas a discreet scheme will make them feel comfortable and able to move in, even if it's not completely to their taste.

As you make decisions about the components of your neutral scheme, don't forget another important factor—yourself. Choose shades, colors and fabrics that work but also that you enjoy. There's no single "correct" scheme. If you can stick to the basic rules, combine your likes and avoid dislikes, you'll end up with a beautiful interior that's a pleasure to live in.

INSPIRATION FROM THE OUTSIDE
This wonderfully clever construction of rich, neutral
shades and rugged, textured materials brings to
mind the complex palette and touch of the forest.
The white sheets are all that is needed to keep the
scheme bright, comfortable and welcoming, despite
the dominance of dark shades.

The Color Palette Directory

THIS EASY-TO-USE CHART ILLUSTRATES THE MAIN COLOR IN EACH OF THE 200 PALETTES. AT A GLANCE YOU CAN SELECT A COLOR THEN TURN TO THE CORRECT PAGE AND DISCOVER HOW TO USE IT EFFECTIVELY IN A PARTICULAR ROOM SCHEME.

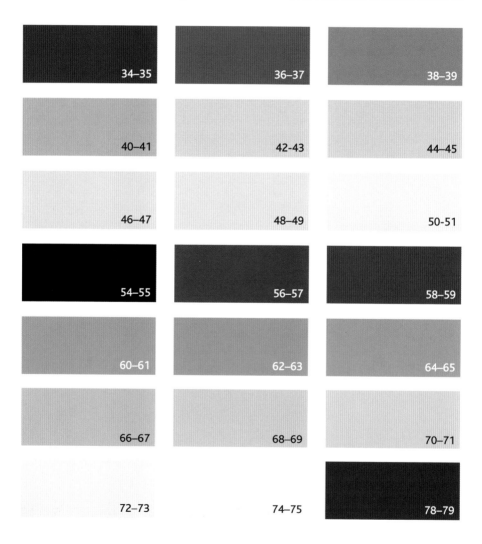

34–35 36–37 38–39
40–41 42-43 44–45
46–47 48–49 50-51
54–55 56–57 58–59
60–61 62–63 64–65
66–67 68–69 70–71
72–73 74–75 78–79

29

80–81

82–83

84–85

86–87

88–89

90–91

92–93

94–95

98–99

100–101

102–103

104–105

106–107

108–109

110–111

112–113

114–115

118–119

120–121

122–123

124–125

126–127

128–129

130–131

132–133

136–137

138–139

140–141

142–143

144–145

146–147

148–149

150–151

154–155

156–157

158–159

160–161

162–163

164–165

166–167

168–169

172–173

174–175

176–177

178–179

180–181

182–183

184–185

186–187

188–189

190–191

194–195

196–197

198–199

200–201

202–203

204–205

206–207

208–209

210–211

212–213

216–217

218–219

220–221

222–223

224–225

226–227

228–229

230–231

234–235

236–237

238–239

240–241

242–243

244–245

246–247

248–249

250–251

252–253

Parisian elegance

Our opening chapter creates sophistication and glamour with color. Long envied as a regal shade, mauve encompasses warm lilacs and subtle lavenders. Think of art deco glamour, tea rooms with white china and martinis served in cut crystal. Adorn your home with decadent textures of velvet and silk and embellished furnishings in classic styles.

Paradise *found*

Rich, intense hues are complemented by nature's neutrals.

Deep plum is a rich and evocative interior color that can add depth and mood to an enclosed or dark space. Warm, passionate and intense, this ripe color makes a great shade for an extravagant feature wall, particularly in a dining room or romantic bedroom.

Warm and soothe deep plum (1) by using it with stone (2) and lichen (3). Woodwork and painted furniture or paneling looks fabulous in these warm tones.

As would be found in nature, plum is complemented by subtle green tones, such as pale sage (4) and soft mint (5). Use these stunning hues as accent shades, mixing tones of green and stone in soft furnishings, rugs or one-off pieces of furniture for a pretty yet cozy and relaxing finish.

Paradise *lost*

Layering deep tones of gasoline blue and deep plum is a brave scheme to take on, but, if used thoughtfully, accent accessories—whether soft furnishings, ceramics or artwork—in dramatic, sensuous gasoline blue complement this shade of plum beautifully and will result in a striking room.

Perfect for a cozy lounge, snug or hideaway or a glamorous dining room.

Paint all walls in deep plum (1), woodwork in light gray (3) and even consider painting the floor or using light gray as a carpet color to contrast with the richness of the plum. Panther gray (2) would work for sofas or throws in a snug or as a large, centralized rug in a dining room.

Mix gasoline blue (4) and charcoal (5) in curtaining and other soft furnishings. These tones lend themselves well to glamorous and sumptuous fabrics such as leather, velvet and silks.

Moulin *rouge*

A deep, delicious and decadently girly group of colors.

This combination is reminiscent of the glory days of the Moulin Rouge, where dancers in deep amethyst silk dresses flaunted themselves and cavorted together through the night. The palette captures much of the romance of early 20th Century France that was evident in the club's decor.

Amethyst (1) is a deep, regal shade. Use it on bedroom walls for a sensual room, with curtains or drapes of fabric in deep purple (5). Use pretty pinks, like blush (2), and candy (3), for bed linen and accessories.

To bring elegance to the look of the room, paint furniture and woodwork in mushroom (4), which looks best in a matte finish. You could also use mushroom for an accent wall if amethyst is too overpowering for the whole room.

Finally, bring deep purple back into the room in an accent piece, be that a throw for the bed or a single upholstered chair.

Powder *room*

This playful collection of colors are inspired by the fun and glamour of the 1950s. The cosmetic-colored accents work well with the depth of the amethyst, and successfully complement juicy plum and the warm brown of deep chestnut. This scheme works well in a lounge or snug as well as a bedroom.

A vintage palette inspired by the 1950s.

Upholstered furniture in plum (4) looks amazing next to amethyst (1); pick a fabric with a slight sheen, such as a chenille or velvet. In a bedroom, upholster an oversized headboard in plum or in a living area, do the same for the sofa. Pick deep chestnut (5) and dusky pink (2) for scatter cushions, perhaps in different textures, or combine the colors in a rug.

Keep flooring and the main curtains or shades more neutral, using hemp (3) to give balance to the scheme.

Understated *elegance*

Embrace the beauty of Art Nouveau with pretty, fresh colors.

The Art Noveau movement, like many design styles, sought to harmonize its forms, and this color scheme seeks to do the same. The fresh, subtle tints of this palette are perfect for a stylish entrance hall or a light, bright drawing room.

1

2

3

4

5

Paneling looks fabulous in a hallway, especially when painted in heritage cream (2). Use dusk (1) as a richer complementary wall color above the paneling for a striking overall effect.

Incorporate slate (4) into the soft furnishings, and experiment with texture, perhaps with some full-length silk curtains, highlighted with warm sand (5) and fresh green (3) in the details or accessories, such as fringes, cushions or vases.

Architectural *influence*

This serious, contemporary palette is crying out for a modern apartment or beautifully proportioned Georgian house—these timeless colors will work well in almost any room. Take inspiration from architectural elements, such as truffle gray and dark steel.

A masculine, pared-down, but highly sophisticated color story.

1

2

3

Paint the walls in dusk (1). For a softer and warmer feel, use rose-cream (4) as the color for flooring.

Upholster furniture in truffle gray (5), using a rich chenille or velvet for a striking and bespoke look and a luxurious texture.

4

Add high gloss or painted furniture in steel (2) or truffle gray, and use all tones, including silver-stone (3), in curtains, shades, cushions and rugs.

5

Elegant *cosmo style*

Team neutrals with mauves for a warm and inviting scheme.

Keep things simple and grown-up with rich toffee and chocolate colors mixed with muted mauves. The delicious, creamy feel of this color combination will help you to create a sumptuous, relaxed feel, perfect for a beautiful bedroom or cozy living area.

1

2

3

Intensify the beauty of mink (1) walls with furniture in walnut or wengé or painted in warm tones of bitter chocolate (5). If using this scheme in a bedroom, inject some drama by painting a feature wall behind the bed in damson (4) or use it as an upholstery fabric for a large, deluxe headboard.

4

5

Khaki (2) and eggshell (3) are beautiful neutrals that can be mixed in using cotton or linen bedding and soft accessories. Use natural floor coverings such as coir or seagrass in khaki to give this scheme a colonial edge.

Art *Nouveau*

The Art Nouveau movement in architecture and design used highly stylized, organic forms as inspiration. In furniture, architecture, art and everyday design, hues from all aspects of nature were used. A calming and soothing tone, mink is reminiscent of the Art Nouveau period.

A sophisticated look that remains pretty and delicate.

1

2

3

Fabrics in pink clay (4) and deep lavender (5), used to upholster furniture and for curtains in a large drawing room or open-plan living space, will tone beautifully with mink (1) colored walls. Against this backdrop, paint cupboards, woodwork or shelving in limestone (2), which would also work well as a painted floor or carpet.

4

5

Accessorize with cushions in limestone, perhaps in silk or Chenille fabric, and large ceramic bowls or artworks in heather (3) and deep lavender.

Stimulating, *warm and sensual*

Stunning colors for a grand entrance or impressive staircase.

Mention the word French gray and you are thrown into an elegant mindset; imagine lounging on a chaise longue, drinking a martini served in a beautiful cut-crystal glass. French gray works just about anywhere, but these selected colors are perfect for a large entrance hall.

1

2

3

To give an old staircase a new lease on life, paint the spindles, treads and risers in ivory (2), but define the handrail in a deeper color, such as mushroom (3), or a real wood finish, such as oak.

4

Add a runner to the stairs in a stripe that combines mushroom (3) deep lilac (4), and raspberry (5).

5

Paint chairs and picture rails in French gray (1), as well as the walls for maximum contemporary glamour. Add curtains, cushions and accessories in any combination of all five colors.

Grown-up *opulence*

The glamour and impact of this scheme is destined for a super-modern kitchen or open-plan living space, however, the palette would also translate into a bedroom setting. In an open-plan, contemporary conversion or new build you should have fun with color and not be afraid to go for it.

Uncompromised luxury, full of tactile experiences and fabrics.

For ultimate impact against the warmth of French gray (1), put in a kitchen with cupboards and units finished in high-gloss purple (3) and sleek and shiny black (4) granite countertops. Silver gray (5) accessories and appliances and other utilitarian items in chrome will zing the colors to life.

In a living area, choose simple stripes or bold patterns in bitter chocolate (2) and purple for soft furnishings, with a background or base color of French gray.

Evening *promise*

A masculine group of colors with feminine undertones.

Masculine meets feminine and warm meets cool in this scheme, yet while the cool tones of royal navy and steel blue contrast with the warmer components of the palette, all seem to work in harmony. This moody and subtle selection would suit a study or drawing room.

1

2

3

4

5

Paint the walls in graceful heather (1) for a beautiful base from which to work.

Subdue the pinky purple highlights of heather with heavy, full-length drapes in dark stone (2) and steel blue (3), and use either steel blue or dark stone as the main upholstery fabric for sofas or chairs. Accessorize with royal navy (5) and steel blue vases and lamp bases.

Use pale lilac (4) and heather for cushions and throws to lift the scheme.

Mineral *spa*

Well known were the healing and healthful benefits of spas to those wealthy enough to take respite in them in the late 19th and early 20th centuries. The colors of natural minerals in rock and crystal forms vary greatly—why not take inspiration from these and create your own spa?

Light some candles, run a bath and take time to relax.

1

2

3

Paint bathroom walls in heather (1) and tongue and groove and bathroom furniture in rich, warm mulberry (5) or fresh, calming marble (3).

Use mulberry and blueberry (4) as inspirational colors for tiles. For a more subtle scheme, you could look at natural slate. Use mirrors to capitalize on any natural light.

4

5

Decorate the bathroom by adding accessories and thick, fluffy towels in refreshing marble and sulfur blue (2).

Grecian *inspired*

Bold blue details to brighten a neutral kitchen.

Early 20th-century fashion designer Mariano Fortuny's "Delphos" dresses were inspired by Ancient Greek clothing and drapery. Made from finely pleated silk, his designs and the simplicity of his style were hugely popular with the rich artistic elite of the day, and this scheme pays homage to him.

1

2

3

4

5

Use this wonderful color combination to adorn your kitchen or dining room. Use soft iris (1) for the majority of your kitchen units, but if you have a larger kitchen paint a stand-alone or island unit in subtle marble (2). Add countertops in mid-oak (3). Paint the largest feature wall in dusty blue (5) and the rest in subtle marble.

If you have space, include a mid-oak dining table and match with gasoline blue (4) upholstered chairs. Don't forget about the finer details of dinnerware: mix different serving dishes in soft iris, dusty blue and subtle marble.

La *Belle Époque*

French for "the beautiful era," the late 19th-century movement of Belle Époque was ostentatious and for the wealthy. All about decadence, it presented a plethora of decorative accessories, such as delicate parasols, feathered hats and beautiful ribboned gloves.

A period of affluence and accessories reborn in this scheme.

1

2

3

For a truly beautiful bedroom, paint walls in soft iris (1). Choose French-boudoir-style furniture painted in rich cream (2). Go for fancy scrolling Baroque beds and perfectly formed armoires, because the intense detail of this style of furniture will look classic and understated when painted. Upholster the headboard or cover an old chair or chaise longue in dusky pink (3) and blueberry (4), and use fern (5) as an accent color for cushions and small accessories.

4

5

This scheme can be made lighter by painting the flooring in rich cream or richer by carpeting the floor in blueberry.

THE COLOR PALETTE DIRECTORY

Dynamic *deco glamour*

Art Deco style: elegant, functional and, above all, modern.

This glamorous movement was the birthplace of Modernism. Opulent and lavish, art deco was an amalgamation of styles—details were geometric and images stylized. Inspired by the essence of this movement, this scheme is suited to an open-plan living space with high ceilings and architectural details.

1

2

3

Use mauve (1) to cover walls in an open living space. Offset mauve's delicate color with masculine greens and grays. Metal finishes such as chrome and steel played a big part in Deco design. Use steel blue (2) for furniture and chrome for any metal detailing.

Create a striking geometric fireplace or add furniture tops in marble (3).

4

5

Add statement pieces of furniture in bold purple (5) and muted jade blue (4).

Vintage *style*

Vintage styles constantly evolve and grow, so always keep an eye out for one-off pieces of pretty vintage fabric, statement pieces of furniture, or interesting prints or pictures. Combine various colors and textures, pattern with plain, silk with cotton and wood with mirror and plastic.

A subdued palette with a selection of your favorite vintage pieces.

1

2

3

Paint walls in mauve (1) and carpet or paint floors a shade darker in purple flora (2). Pick taupe (4) as the main color for curtains or the largest items of furniture, and charcoal (5) for other pieces. Choose good-quality, tactile fabrics for furniture and curtains—they have to feel luxurious to stop a vintage scheme looking shabby rather than chic.

4

5

Add striped rugs and throws in buttermilk (3) and purple flora to complete the look.

Pretty *in pink*

Soft pink tones perfect for a girl's bedroom.

Pink can be overpowering used to excess, but it makes for a beautiful, almost fragrant bedroom when thoughtfully combined with these accent colors. Straight off the cosmetic counter, these playful pinks and violets cry out to be used in a girl's bedroom.

1

2

3

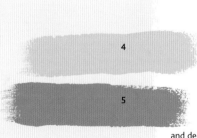

4

5

Paint the walls in pinked gray (1). Pick out fixed features, such as a fireplace or fitted wardrobes, in milkshake (3).

For the windows, use coffee (4) shades and delicate flowing voiles or silks as drapes in petal (2) and gorgeous pansy pink (5).

It's all about the details when you're being girly, so add crystal handles and decorative accessories in pansy pink. Flooring can be pure white floorboards or, for a warmer feel, carpet in coffee.

Timeless *romance*

Take inspiration from the pretty colors of makeup, but refine the pinks and purples into muted pinky grays and neutrals. Use bold reds and pinks and purples to accent the scheme, be that with artwork, a single vase or a simple, bold cushion.

A more mature palette for a romantic yet contemporary look.

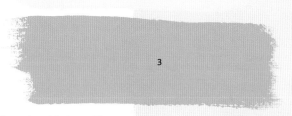

1

2

3

4

5

Complementing pinked gray (1) walls, paint or paper a feature wall in lavender (3).

Keep sofas and chairs to a neutral gray (2) in a simple woven, textured fabric.

Add lamps and diffused lighting with simple glass bases and shades in either lavender, or pinked gray.

Use chalky coral (4) and/or oxblood (5) in a one-off canvas, floor vase or single chair to set the scheme off.

Modern art

Flirting between cooler blue-grays, greens
and warm stony neutrals, gray is a moody
contemporary tone. Associate these palettes with
geometric shapes, steel, glass and metal. Highlight
muddy creams, murky whites and gritty grays with
hints of rich pigments or acid brights. Use these
pages to conjure up images of modern interiors,
utilitarian and functional in style.

Primary *modern*

Take on Mondrian's lines in a bold, fun playroom.

The great French painter Piet Mondrian is synonymous with the concept of primary colors with black. His paintings of straight black lines and "pods" of red, yellow and blue have been replicated in design and interiors many times. Use this color selection to interpret the style in your own way.

Paint opposing walls or panels on walls in a combination of primary red (2), bright yellow (3) and blue (4). Mask out lines in coal black (1) to separate the color panels. Put a practical rubber floor down in coal black and punctuate this with small rugs in the three primary colors.

To keep the look fresh and clean, paint baseboards and ceilings in pure white (5). As an added treat for the children, paint reachable rectangular squares with blackboard paint.

Lively *simple lines*

The modern artist Wassily Kandinsky was obsessed with color and form, and his abstract paintings from the early part of the 20th century are lively explosions of colorful abstracts. His shapes and colors interject and overlap in a very free and almost haphazard way.

Layer a muted palette of grays and ochers for a luxurious bedroom.

Coordinate the furniture in the bedroom from the bed to the wardrobe doors in coal black (1) gloss or black glass. Paint the walls in chalk (3) and carpet the floor in rich yellow ocher (2). If you can find a good retro wallpaper with ochers, purples and blacks, use this to paper the bed-side wall of the room. Upholster the headboard in decadent coal black silk, with chalk silk buttoning.

Finally, layer decorative bedding in shades of yellow ocher, verde (4) and purple (5).

Punchy *pop art*

*Be inspired by the
Swinging Sixties.*

Synonymous with the new, exciting and radical trends of the time, this 1960s palette is based around bold and bright hues. These punchy colors would translate well in a large, high-ceilinged room.

1

2

3

Paint the largest wall of the room in minted white (2) to give a focal point and the rest of the walls in pure white (3), and then choose a carpet, wood floor or rubber floor in charcoal (1).

4

Add bold pieces of furniture in sunset orange (4) and other smaller items, such as cushions or vases, in pale lilac (5).

5

Finally, accessorize the white walls by adding pop art prints on canvas to bring the whole scheme together.

Artist's *studio*

If you've ever been lucky enough to see an artist at work, you'll know they have palettes, jars, half-finished paintings and brushes everywhere. It's organized chaos, but a cozy and welcoming space.

A neutral base is a blank canvas to work within.

1

2

3

Recreate an artist's paradise using found objects and quirky antique pieces of furniture.

Use charcoal (1) for the walls in a cozy sitting room, and carpet the floor in creamy buff (2).

Add different wood finishes, such as dark and medium oak (5, 4), for example, with furniture and picture frames. You may also want to add a framed mirror in the same wood finish. Moss green (3) makes an excellent choice for upholstered chairs and other soft furnishing items.

4

5

Making *an impression*

Use color freely and embrace Impressionism.

The late 19th-century Impressionist art movement that began in Paris changed the face of painting forever. Characterized by ordinary scenes as subject matter, visible brushstrokes, unusual visual angles and an emphasis on light and its changing qualities, it was at one with nature.

This pretty palette of soft, timeless accents will work in many applications but would be perfect for a kitchen.

Make your countertops and wall tiles granite (1), and complement them with ash white (2) painted cupboards and ceramic crackle-glaze knobs in morning blue (5). Hints of this blue will lift color from the granite.

For the ceiling and remaining woodwork use pure white (3), and paint the remaining wall space in lavender white (4). Accessorize with dinnerware in any of these colors.

Painting *the weather*

The great British artist Joseph William Turner painted spectacular re-creations of natural weather conditions, such as sunlight, storms, rain and fog. There is such a depth of color in his work; even in his scenes of shipwrecks and storms there are pockets of pinks, oranges, and bright blues.

Use Turner's moody colors in the hallway of a traditional house.

Interpret Turner's style in your own way to create a stunning entrance and hallway.

Use a natural stone or slate floor in granite (1) through the entrance and hall of your house. Paint blue slate (4) below the chair rail and lighter natural stone (3) above it.

Paint baseboards and woodwork in white stone (2), and carpet the stairs with a runner in salmon pink (5) for a splash of color. Alternatively, inject this color by adding the odd picture frame or vase in the same shade.

Restrained *fresco detailing*

*A blush palette of
plaster-inspired colors.*

Painting frescoes is a highly skilled and difficult job. Many of the greatest paintings in Europe, such as the ceiling of the Sistine Chapel, are decorated in frescoes. Painted on a thin layer of wet plaster, pigments sink into this layer so that the plaster itself becomes the medium.

1

2

3

This plaster-inspired scheme is perfect for a bedroom or lounge.

Use panther gray (1) as a base color for furniture; this could be painted flat or as a contemporary grayed-oak finish or used to paint walls. Alternatively, paint walls in plaster (4) for a warm pink glow and woodwork in oyster (2) for a subtle tonal difference.

4

5

Upholster furniture in minky brown (3) velvet or silk, and find a simple but elegant patterned fabric for curtains or shades in a mix of Venetian pink (5) and minky brown.

Wild *Fauvism*

Inspired by the French word *fauve*, meaning "wild animals," the Fauvists went wild with color. Fauvism progressed from Impressionism, with simplified designs in bright colors, characterized by artists such as Henri Matisse and Raoul Dufy.

Blues and purples feature heavily in the Fauvists' colorful paintings.

1

2

3

Use bold color washes, as Dufy did, in a grown-up lounge. Use panther gray (1) as the wall color, bar one, which will form the backdrop of the scheme.
Cover this wall in panels of lavender (3) silk. Carpet the lounge in white lilac (2), using a carpet with silk or a slight sheen running through it if possible.

4

5

Frame the entrance to the lounge and any external windows or glass doors with tall, elegant planters in deep ocean (5), planted with simple structural plants or cacti. Curtain with full-length silks that pool on the carpet in Chinese blue (4) and lavender.

Drawing *the outside in*

A combination of colors based on the great outdoors.

In the 1880s, large numbers of British artists began to visit Cornwall in England, and the pretty fishing village of Newlyn soon became home to a school of artists, who started the "plein air" movement. Translating as "open air," it encouraged artists to paint outdoors.

1

2

3

The silvery undertones in buttercup cream (2) will complement a lead (1) carpet or natural stone floor. Use it as your wall color, and team with sackcloth (5) as a woven, heavy linen for curtains, with pastel white (4) sheer beneath.

4

Choose sackcloth cotton or chenille as upholstery fabric for luxurious sofas, and add plenty of scatter cushions in duck egg (3), in different textures.

5

Natural, *organic arrangement*

Sculptural forms can be simply beautiful. From Henry Moore's huge abstractions of organic shapes to a tiny Art Deco nude bronze. A sculpture is a piece to be admired in its own right. With this in mind, this palette would suit a room for an indoor pool, where the main focus is the water itself.

A truly superb color combination to rival any spa hotel.

1

2

3

The fabulous color combination of clean, sleek, modern neutrals shown here will help you to make the most of this area.

Tile the pool area in lead (1), with an edging around the actual pool of marble (4), and paint the unglazed walls in dark stone (2).

4

For around the pool area select loungers and furniture in dark wood similar to woodland brown (3), and add fabric or towels in ink (5).

5

Collector's *character*

Make a real feature of a collection of paintings or photographs.

For something different, choose a selection of differently sized picture frames, but to keep them looking like they belong together use bronze (4) as a finished color on all of them. Paint the walls in sackcloth. The bronze finish of the frames will lift out of the sackcloth walls.

1

2

3

Keep the flooring in this room bright and light by painting boards or carpeting in ivory (2).

Find odd pieces of wooden furniture in dark oak or walnut (5), keeping the same type of color or finish but playing with scales and sizes.

4

For your upholstery and curtains, use a combination of stripes, florals and plain cottons in sage (3), sackcloth (1), and ivory. Accessorize with further combinations of these accent colors.

5

Decorating *in Deco*

In many Art Deco images and interiors of the 1920s and 1930s, the main colors are pale, sensual backdrop colors, such as grays, creams, beiges and ivories. Contrasting bolder colors or materials were then employed to give dramatic effect. Why not do the same in your interior?

Deco-inspired schemes for a sunroom or garden room.

Splash out on a beautiful old sandstone (4) or travertine floor. There probably won't be much wall space, but what there is can be painted in sackcloth (1).

Buy contemporary rattan or upholstered chairs and sofas in ivory blush (3), and make simple additional cushions in café au lait (2) and charcoal (5).

Finally, add contemporary large planters in charcoal and fill with a suitably hardy, slow-growing plant.

Modern *materials*

A design and color scheme inspired by the iconic Barcelona chair.

The Barcelona chair is renowned for its perfect style, form, comfort and elegance. Mies van der Rohe, the German architect, originally designed the chair for the king and queen of Spain to sit on at the 1929 Barcelona World Exposition.

1

2

3

Execute this scheme in a formal lounge or a large, grand entrance hall or staircase.

At the heart of your chosen room place two Barcelona chairs symmetrically next to each other, in black-brown (3). Sit these on a subtle ivory blush (4) carpet or tiled floor.

4

5

Paint or paper the walls in concrete (1), and find a silk or cotton sateen in copper (5) or milk chocolate (2) to make simple, full-length drapes. Accessorize with large ceramic floor vases, planters or sculptures in black-brown and copper.

Earth *colors*

Before paints were chemically produced, earth colors were used as a paint medium. These earth colors were natural pigments found in their original state in the earth and include red ochers, various shades of yellows and browns and terre vert, a grayish green.

Hues from the earth to create warmth and comfort.

1

2

3

Implement this earthy scheme in a living space—a relaxed and informal zone where you can read, chill out or simply curl up and snooze the afternoon away.

Concrete (1) is a good base gray that can be warmed up by the soft accents of wet clay (2) and pale sand (3). Opt for a natural carpet and simple curtains or shades in a weighty cotton print of wet clay, pale sand and water (4).

4

5

Upholster sofas in natural indigo (5) cotton and add big cotton cushions in pale sand and water. Add bookcases and pictures to complete your retreat.

African *art*

Bold colors and animal prints for an African vision.

One of the hallmarks of Art Deco design was the rich melting pot of cultural influences. The excitement of the African safari, high on the list of "must-sees" for the Art Deco traveler, was recreated in the home through striking items such as a sofa covered in zebra stripe or leopard print upholstery or a primitive tribal-inspired ebony stool.

1

2

3

Why not recreate your own cultural vision? Use clay (1) as your neutral backdrop; paint your walls in this color and then add simple pale sea green (3) curtains on barely black (2) poles. Upholster an old chair in animal print, and sit it next to a painted trunk in earth red (5).

4

5

To accessorize, place mustard (4) vases symmetrically next to each other on a shelf or on a piece of furniture, then bring all the bold, earthy tones together in a striped rug.

Taken *from Egypt*

A mystical and regal land that has inspired numerous cultures and movements over time, the ancient Egyptian civilization has it roots in the fertile land around the Nile. Combine the natural colors of the land with the colors of the sky for a bold, fun, yet grown-up scheme that works particularly well in an older child's bedroom.

A scheme inspired by the natural landscape of ancient Egypt.

1

2

3

Paint the main walls in clay (1), then paint one wall or into the alcoves around a chimney breast in Nile blue (3) with peacock (2) on the actual breast.

To adorn the walls, spray wide picture frames in palm (5) and fill with photos, collage boards or abstract prints. Make simple blinds in palm and peacock stripes, and paint cupboards, storage chests or shelving in old gold (4).

4

5

Rolling *landscapes*

Recreate the richness and vitality of the outdoors inside.

The region of Tuscany in central Italy is considered the birthplace of the Renaissance movement and has a rich artistic heritage. This scheme is reminiscent of the lush Italian landscape filled with cypress trees, olive groves and vineyards and soaked in glowing sunshine.

1

2

3

To conjure up the beauty of Tuscany, implement this palette in a lounge or dining room.

Cover the walls in baked clay (1) and add sofas upholstered in rich, velvety olive (4) with the odd statement chair in corn (2).

Put in a warm, natural oak floor with a couple of rugs in striped emerald gray (5) and Tuscan yellow (3).

4

5

Accessorize with cushions and vases or ceramic bowls in any one of these selected colors.

Renaissance *Italy*

An easily translated group of colors, the base of three neutrals is highlighted by pinky reds. Renaissance means "rebirth," or to be born again, and is a word synonymous with change. When giving a room a makeover or a new lease on life you must have a plan or scheme in mind.

Warm neutrals teamed with red and pink accents.

1

2

3

For a bathroom or en suite, choose a rich, warm travertine floor and wall tiles in baked clay (1), and choose a stone mosaic border in a mix of baked clay, buttermilk (2) and dark stone (3). This simple application of neutrals will look stunning. Paint any remaining walls in buttermilk.

4

5

Use garnet (5) as a painted frame for a mirror on the wall or a vase on a window ledge, and finish with a mix of garnet, plaster pink (4) and dark stone towels.

Watercolor *wash*

Soft and delicate watercolors for a bedroom.

Watercolors are renowned for their delicacy and translucency. Choose your favorite watercolor painting and you'll find in it a plethora of playful colors. Examine the way they lap over each other, creating new colors and merging softly to form a beautiful series of fluid marks.

1

2

3

In a bedroom, you can be soft and subtle with fabrics and colors and create similar watercolor effects within the room.

Try washing the walls with pastel white (1) and mint (2) for a painterly finish. Drape sheers at the windows in layers of buttermilk (4) that can flap in the wind and diffuse the sunlight. Accent with sunshine tones of peach pink (3) and warm yellow (5).

4

5

Find your inner artisan and take painterly inspiration by "decorating" a chair or chest of drawers with a simple pattern in peach pink, warm yellow and mint.

Moody *blues*

Blue is one color that can be both masculine and feminine, and can work monochromatically. Tranquil blues within a color scheme lighten the mood, and darker shades can be used for dramatic effect. This undulating range of steel blues will work well in a bright and airy adult room.

Experiment with a range of both deep and light blues.

1

2

3

Paint the walls in pastel white (1). This will help to make the room feel light and airy and thus spacious. Keep all upholstery, curtains and main soft furnishings in blue slate (4).

Accessorize selectively with the remaining ice blue (2), fresh blue (3) and storm blue (5), perhaps by adding a pair of large floor vases in ice blue, for example, or a striped throw in all three. Finally, finish with large, plump cushions of varying textures in storm blue.

4

5

Drawing *from charcoal*

Tones of gray for a serious, sophisticated, contemporary look.

Charcoal is an age-old drawing material. Its flexibility means you can use it to make fine lines and to "tone" or cover large sections of a drawing surface. Playing with tones of colors, such as charcoal, and teaming them with lighter neutrals will help you to create a striking interior.

1

2

3

Color has an immediate impact on the human eye, and the atmosphere of any room is set by the dominant shades. This scheme would work well in a modern open-plan apartment.

4

5

Choose pieces of furniture in muted basil (4) and black leather (5) to sit in this graphic environment. Pick out accent walls with panther gray (3) that will tone against chalk white (1) as an overall base color.

Use tones of soft gray (2) for carpet and soft furnishings in a range of textures, and add strong black and white graphic prints and mirrors to finish the look.

Chalky *whites*

Neutrals are key in creating light and airy rooms, and will help you make the most of any light source. All of these selected colors have a similar "strength," so the overall feel will be harmonious and relaxing. These bright, clean colors will work well in a cheery kitchen or sunny bedroom.

Chalky pastels that feel as fresh as a summer's day.

1

2

3

Lime white (2) is the perfect choice for painted furniture and fitted cupboards. Paint the walls in chalk white (1). If it's practical to have a wooden floor, paint it in chalk also, to keep the whole feel of the room fresh and light.

4

Find a pretty floral fabric in sackcloth (5) and light brick (4) that has hints of either lime white or pale peach (3), and use it for upholstery or drapes. To bring contrast into the scheme, use different textures and materials and accessorize with vases or ceramic bowls in any of these beautiful accent colors.

5

Stunning
seascapes

Crashing waves, deserted beaches, moody blues and stony grays; nature is our greatest source of inspiration, without us even realizing it. The sea holds a plethora of colors and tones. Pick out varying tones from shells on a beach, sandy neutrals to complement grayish blues and the highlights and low-lights of a stormy sky.

Midnight *blue*

A treasure trove of coastal color.

Seascapes have always been an inspiration. The clear, shallow coastal waters of the tropical sea are home to an explosion of natural color combinations, which you can recreate by playing midnight against neon yellow and coral orange.

1

2

3

4

5

If you're feeling artistic, paint walls in a child's bedroom or playroom in midnight (1), leaving a blank area or wall on which to create an underwater mural using neon yellow (4), coral orange (5), marine (3) and aqua (2). Paint or carpet the floor in marine and add large, colorful rugs.

Choose bright coral orange for the lamp shades, and paint furniture in aqua and neon yellow for a bright, fun look.

Deep *blue sea*

Blues are known for their calming and soothing properties and are a favorite for bedrooms, bathrooms and studies. However, they can look cold and unwelcoming, so make sure your blue isn't too chilly by choosing one with a warm undertone or by combining it with warm accent colors.

Use the warmth of natural stone to complement blue.

This palette will work well in a sleek, contemporary bathroom.

Use midnight (1) as a wall color in a bathroom tiled with natural stone in warm heritage cream (4) and gray stone (5). White says "clean" and "fresh," perfect for a bathroom scheme, so add pure white (2) limestone basins and fixtures.

Keep it simple and add towels and accessories in morning mist (3) and midnight.

Stormy *weather*

A steely selection of colors for a classic study.

The range of blue through gray that can be seen in the sea and sky is incomprehensible. Nature offers us a plethora of wondrous color combinations that are replicated in design over and over, and in a small space dark colors can work well if executed correctly.

1

2

3

4

5

Paint walls in storm blue (1) and woodwork in pale gray (2), including any detail, such as fireplace mantels or shelving. Dress the windows in drapes or shades in either pale gray, or pale sea green (5).

Upholster an easy chair in a traditional floral incorporating storm cloud (4) and pale sea green. Add simple cushions in any one of the palette's accent colors and add mirrored and steel blue (3) accessories, such as candlesticks, vases and picture frames, to finish.

Driftwood *art*

There is something deeply romantic about collecting driftwood from the beach and imagining its origins. You can also source ready-made driftwood products that master craftsmen have fashioned into furniture, mirrors and decorative sculptures.

Bleached accent colors to mimic driftwood.

To create a perfect backdrop for driftwood accessories, paint walls in storm blue (1) and paper a single feature wall in an elegant, flowing pattern of storm blue and morning mist (4).

Keep furniture light, either with a bleached or light wood finish and find a large striped rug in morning mist and shell (2). Upholster furniture in pale sand (3) and add scatter cushions in storm blue, morning mist, dark wood (5) and shell in varying textures to complete.

New England *style*

A homely, comfortable scheme that is perfect for family living.

Appliqué cushions, heart details on hand-forged iron hooks, decorative tinplate signs, peg boards, wood-clad walls and shuttered windows all scream New England style. Have fun implementing this scheme in a family living room.

1

2

3

4

5

Incorporate steel (1) into every aspect of the scheme; using it to paint wood shutters could provide the main focus. Paint the walls in blue haze (3), and then decorate them with tin signs and pictures of boats and sea views in wood (5) and steel painted frames.

Cover sofas in a heavy damask fabric in steel and accent with cotton and velvet cushions in baby blue (2) and blue haze. Add simple shaker-style furniture in wood, and upholster a chair or footstool in an American-inspired stripe of red flag (4), steel and white.

Striking *vistas*

The similar-toned colors that make up this palette are yet another way for you to bring the beauty of a seascape into your own home. In order to take full advantage of a great view, maximize windows with simple dressings and use planters inside to draw your eye out to the vista beyond.

Make the most of a beautiful sea view with a pared-down interior.

1

2

3

In a garden room or sunroom, paint what wall area there is in steel (1), and paint all woodwork in pure white (2). In this kind of room the windows are usually the main feature, so take care when dressing them. If you have short windows use simple roller shades in steel, and for larger, tall windows choose a fabric in steel and mocha (3) and use either for curtains or Roman shades.

4

5

Sum up this scheme with black (4) leather and chrome gray (5) furniture. Lastly, frame the main view with black planters filled with stunning lush green plants.

Rugged *landscape*

Bring the minerals of the earth into a modern bathroom.

When talking of seascapes, it is usually the sea itself that springs to mind, but we mustn't forget the sand, cliffs and jagged rocks that border the coast. Natural stone and marble cut from the earth are simply the most beautiful materials to use in a bathroom.

1

2

3

Base your scheme around a natural marble, and tile the floor and a feature wall in ice (2) and pastel gray (3). Paint the remaining wall space in flint (1).

Add real glamour with a traditional claw-foot tub, and paint the outside and feet in flint.

4

5

Zap color into this muted theme with zingy textiles. If you have a large window, curtain it in a silk organza in citrine (4) and mid-blue (5), otherwise find a cotton print for a Roman blind. Choose towels and a bath mat in mid-blue to give the room a fresh, modern twist.

Coastal *lines*

The salted air and harsh coastal winds are responsible for the weathered rock and tumbling landscape that make up coastlines. Think of the way the white face of a cliff envelops the sea edge in an elegant, undulating line, and employ this simplicity in an entrance hall.

Seashore simplicity for a light, fresh entrance hall.

1

2

3

Use flint (1) as a paper or paint beneath a chair rail, then paper above it with a classic design in pearl gray (2) and raw silk (3). Keep all woodwork and furniture in the same paint finish of raw silk.

If curtains or shades are required, stick to a plain silk or voile in mauve (4). If curtains aren't a necessary addition, shade a pair of lamps in mauve instead.

4

5

Finally, add a welcoming, homely touch using cut flowers in traditional cut-glass vases, choosing a contrasting, fresh color such as pale honey (5).

Côte d'Azur

Inspired by the coastal villages of Provence in the south of France.

Transport yourself to the pretty white villages drenched in sunshine, surrounded by lavender fields and overlooking the deep blue sea of the Côte d'Azur coast. Import this beauty by utilizing this scheme in a living or dining room.

1

2

3

Use Paris blue (1) as the main recurring color in textiles and upholstery, using a selection of florals, stripes, dots and plain fabrics and as the color for one accent wall. Paint the remaining walls and floor simply in limestone (2).

4

5

Paint a single piece of furniture, such as an old dresser, bookcase or wardrobe, in matte gray (3).

To accent this scheme beautifully use wine (5) as the color for a pair of accessories, such as lampshades or vases, before adding fresh plants in dark olive (4) and wine.

Mediterranean *breeze*

Give your room a continental twist, taking inspiration from the vibrancy of the terra-cottas and blues of Mediterranean style. The color contrasts of this scheme will work exceptionally well in a large family or farmhouse kitchen.

A bold, lively new look for a family kitchen.

1

2

3

Pastel-colored cabinets create a homely atmosphere, so paint units in Paris blue (1) and sky (2). Contrast these blues with brown mustard (5) walls and rustic wooden countertops in sand (4).

Use a bright, striped fabric that brings the blues and browns together for Roman shades, and dot authentic Mediterranean kitchen pieces, for example, in wood, earthenware or terra-cotta, around the room. A rustic wine rack will easily feel at home here too.

4

5

All *calm at sea*

Seductive sea shades for a sumptuous bedroom.

An aquatic palette of bright blues and greens accompanies an eclectic mix of patterns and fabrics. Use this scheme in a master bedroom and transport yourself to a sun-drenched balcony nestled above the water's edge.

1

2

3

4

5

Seduce slate blue (1) walls with an oversized headboard in sea (5), using a sensual fabric—perhaps embroidered or embellished—with plenty of impact. Furnish the room with painted furniture in chalky cream (2), and paint floorboards with driftwood (3).

Choose a luxurious sea kelp (4) and sea (5) bedspread and some decorative cushions in sea kelp. For curtains or shades keep it simple and either choose wooden Venetian blinds or simple voiles in chalky cream, or use sea for floor-length drapes in a natural silk.

Eastern *promise*

The lotus has its roots in mud and grows upward through the water, where its petals open out into a beautiful flower. At night the flower closes and disappears underwater, until dawn when it rises and opens again. Featuring extensively in the art of ancient Egypt, it was a symbol of beauty and purity.

A stunning lounge inspired by the colors of the lotus flower.

1

2

3

For a refined and svelte lounge, paint walls in slate blue (1) and carpet the room in haze (2), then use mud (3) for simple Roman shades and as a main upholstery fabric.

4

Cover a pair of footstools or small chairs in lotus (4), and cushion the main seating areas using fabrics in a mix of jewel (5), haze, slate blue and lotus.

5

Add a pair of ethnic sculptures or vases either side of a fireplace or chimney breast for a hint of Eastern influence.

Windswept *dunes*

Bring the outside in with tones of grass green and sand.

The natural colors of the sea and its surrounding landscape feature prominently in this springlike scheme. This palette is simple, understated and subtle, using a warm palette of clean colors to freshen the room, and will work well in a light and airy kitchen.

1

2

3

Give a kitchen a fresh look by painting the walls in ice blue (1) and using dune (3) as a base color for kitchen units and furniture. Brighten up windows with simple roller shades in golden sand (2) that will zing off the ice blue walls.

Find a chunky oak trestle table with oak benches and add cushioned seat pads upholstered in a mix of rushes (4) and stream green (5). Be creative with your plates and bowls, and bring greens and blues to life in the day-to-day practical accessories you use.

4

5

Coastal *retreat*

As reiterated throughout this book, neutrals are great at creating the illusion of a light, airy atmosphere and thus can make the smallest of rooms feel spacious, although sometimes more is needed. In an awkward-shaped entrance or hallway, use this playful selection of colors to make a comfortable space.

Clever colors and ideas to make the most of awkward spaces.

1

2

3

In quirky or old houses you may need to think creatively about how best to use a space. For instance, hallways are often large but not quite large enough to make into a "room" or a defined, usable space.

Make use of walls by creating fixed seating with storage boxes or cupboards underneath painted in rose white (2) and set against a backdrop of ice blue (1). Cover the wooden seats with pretty cushions in brown blush (3), rum butter (5) and midnight (4), mixing florals, stripes, embroidered and plain fabrics.

4

5

Boats *in harbor*

A bright, exciting and fun scheme for a boy's room.

Little boys love boats, and this nautical scheme is perfect for a boy's bedroom or playroom. Working in horizontal stripes, paint the top 65 percent of the walls in dusky blue, then, working down, paint the next 20 percent in royal blue and the remaining 15 percent in meadow green (4).

1

2

3

To implement a true nautical style, mix wood and pure white (3) painted furniture throughout the room.

Find fun items to put into the room that are in keeping with the style, such as boat-shaped shelving, a traditional hammock and large model boats.

4

5

Paint the floor in pure white and add funky rugs in dusky blue (1) and seaweed (5). Bed linen can adopt any one or a combination of these colors. To finish, put royal blue (2) shades at the windows with pure white voile drapes.

Weathered *beach huts*

These pastel, bleached colors are not just for sweet, pretty girls' rooms. If used correctly and in a contemporary way, they can have real impact and will create a stunning bedroom for anyone or alternatively, a beautiful lounge.

A pretty blend of perfect pastels to brighten any room.

1

2

3

Hang long granite gray (5) drapes in a heavy woven cotton or velvet at the windows, against the subtle wall color of dusky blue (1). For upholstery, use a combination of silver-cream (2) and bunting pink (3), keeping it neat and unfussy so these pastels don't look too sickly.

4

Carpet in silver-cream and powder blue (4), or choose a woven rug if you have floorboards.

5

Add a striking standard lamp with a dark wood base and a silver-cream shade to sit against the dusky blue walls, and find room for a large powder blue vase or glass ornament.

Colorful *vintage*

An explosion of 1950s vacation color.

Grab a mai tai and go tropical with a scheme that radiates happiness and enjoyment. The bright, cheerful accents of this palette work exceptionally well with tranquil pale ocean and used cleverly will bring your chosen room to life, without overdoing it.

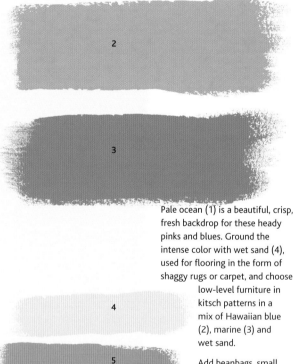

1

2

3

Pale ocean (1) is a beautiful, crisp, fresh backdrop for these heady pinks and blues. Ground the intense color with wet sand (4), used for flooring in the form of shaggy rugs or carpet, and choose low-level furniture in kitsch patterns in a mix of Hawaiian blue (2), marine (3) and wet sand.

4

5

Add beanbags, small upholstered stools or floor cushions in prints and plains in marine and paradise pink (5). Finally, dig out retro lamps, unusual period prints and other 1950s pieces to really bring the scheme together.

Deserted *beach*

An atmospheric bedroom scheme that evokes images of the sun setting over the sea on a winter afternoon. Combining the fresh, light neutrals of the beach with the deepest blue of the ocean and the rich brown of African walnut will help you capture the essence of coastal living, wherever you may live.

A natural palette for your very own beach paradise.

1

2

3

To create a beachy retreat in your home, collect natural objects, interesting shells, stones, driftwood and old crates for effortless chic.

Contrast African walnut (5) furniture against pale ocean (1) walls. Find nautical fabrics, such as stripes and natural linens, in shell (2), cloud (3) and ink (4), and use them to make cushion covers with ties and loose covers for chairs. Give everything a "crafty" edge to complete the concept.

Classic flora

A collection of schemes influenced by the beauty
of flowers. Take inspiration from the colors and
tones found naturally in some of nature's sweetest
flora: violets, lavenders, irises and wisteria. Violets
are creative and have expressive tones that are
sensual, stimulating and emotional. Close your
eyes and imagine the soft, silky texture of a petal,
and interpret this delicate image in your color
scheme and the fabrics you use.

Beauty *of the Amazon*

Degrees of blue-violet create a moody, rich bedroom hideaway.

An undulating green carpet of vegetation punctuated by areas of water, the Amazon is one of the most diverse and unexplored natural environments on the planet. This color scheme takes its inspiration from the mystery of this wondrous area.

1

2

3

Be bold with deep, exotic blackberry (1) on the walls, punctuated by a cloud (2) chair rail and cornice in a matte finish, so the look doesn't become brash. Upholster an oversized headboard in cloud, in a shiny fabric such as velvet or silk.

4

5

For a dazzling explosion of color, curtain in violet (4), letting the sheer weight of the color shine through, rather than using a fussy heading or design. Upholster a chair in Amazon blue (5), choosing a shiny fabric to give the chair impact against the dark walls. Add gray (3) accessories for a sleek finish.

Lakeside *retreat*

This scheme conjures up an image of a log cabin tucked away in a forest and overlooking a moody black lake. A deep, dark scheme such as this is perfect for a dining room that is used predominantly in the evening, and it provides lots of scope for the addition of brighter accents.

A beautiful selection of woodland colors to dine among.

Paint the focal wall—one that is free of features such as windows or doors—in twilight (5) and the others in blackberry (1). To adorn, add artwork to the focal wall in blackberry and gooseberry (3).

Upholster dining chairs in glorious rich moss (4) edged with fern green (2), and follow these greens through to accessories, such as table runners, glassware and candlesticks. Twilight is also a great color to accessorize the room with, and combining it with the other natural hues in this palette will result in a stunning overall look.

Winter *pansies*

Zest up a dark space with the colors of cheery winter pansies.

The pansy is an often overlooked plant, but its petals of white, pink, blue or violet sparkle even on the most overcast of days and can bring pleasure and color to the dull winter months. Take inspiration from these flowers and use them to enliven a dark, dull, tired or small space.

1

2

3

Bring some bold sunshine colors into a child's playroom by painting alternating walls in crocus (4) and hot orange (5). This will lift fantastically off a rich deep violet (1) rubber floor, which is not only soft underfoot but durable and practical as well.

4

5

Into one of the corners of the room suspend a hammock in deep violet, pale violet (3) and lemon cream (2) or a funky plastic hanging chair.

To complete, accessorize with round rugs in crocus and hot orange and furniture painted in lemon cream.

Bluebell *woods*

Spring is a season associated with life and new beginnings, and there is no clearer sign that spring is here than a forest floor carpeted in bluebells. The mass of deep blue-violet lapping at the edges of green grass and punctuated by the dark bark of tree trunks translates into a stunning room scheme.

A spring palette to transform any study.

Paint the walls in deep violet (1) and carpet the room in gray bark (3). Add a Victorian desk in a warm oak or mahogany finish and an old chair upholstered in foliage green (4) leather.

For shades and curtains, keep the look studious and sophisticated; choose a masculine fabric, such as a simple weave or check in gray bark and lavender blue (5).

Finally, make a centerpiece of a striking piece of glass or a large ceramic sculpture in gorgeous bluebell (2).

Nature's *renaissance*

An unusual group of colors with a fresh, contemporary edge.

Although bright and modern, these colors are all drawn from nature. This scheme is perfect for a beach house or cottage on the coast and is sure to promote calm and relaxation wherever you choose to implement it.

1

2

3

Use pure white (2) as a painted floor, and paint walls in regal blue (1); you may want to add random stripes or stars in pure white.

Add deep, comfy sofas in regal blue denim cotton and antique pieces of chunky, deep earth brown (5) furniture, which will work perfectly with the blue and white hues.

4

5

Tease the regal theme by accessorizing with cushions, throws and trinkets in pink peach (3) and hot pink (4).

The *herb garden*

Fresh herbs not only taste fantastic and smell amazing, they also show a diverse range of colors and textures, which are the inspiration behind this group of colors.

Bring the lush richness of the garden into the bedroom.

Regal blue (1), like the leaves of blue basil, can be used as a main color for a truly organic bedroom. Offset the blue with gentle thyme flower (2) as an upholstered headboard and carpet or painted floor.

Frame windows with full drapes of purple sage (4), and add decadent tassels or tiebacks made from crystals in thyme flower. Pile the bed high with cushions in minted blue (5) edged with mustard yellow (3) and purple sage.

Fresh, *bright and lifting*

The mix of cool and warm tones here gives an unexpected edge.

Sometimes you need to be bold in your design choices. If you are ready for a change, try this energizing palette. It would work particularly well in an open-plan living or work space—perhaps a studio or warehouse apartment.

1

2

3

4

5

Paint most of the walls in deep blueberry (1), but pick out a few in gray light (2). Use deep blueberry for large, key items in the room, for example as high-gloss kitchen units, with a countertop in gray light and contrasting aqua white (3) bar stools.

Use a bright rug in citrus tones (4, 5) to define the living or working area of the space, and add dark sofas in deep blueberry.

To finish, pick out individual items in bright colors, for example, a footstool in aqua white or a floor vase in citrus orange (4).

Pretty *pastels*

Pastels don't have to be boring or reserved merely for girls' bedrooms, just make sure you use them in the right finish and application. These colors sit best with natural fabrics and woods, not shiny metal or perfect finishes.

Choose soft pastels for a cozy, private hideaway.

Work the softer side of deep blueberry (1) in a cozy lounge by complementing the walls with brushed cottons for upholstery. Snuggle up in some squashy sofas in sage green (5). Add knitted cushions and throws in pinked gray (4) and delphinium (3) edged with pearl blue (2) buttons.

Use a mix of natural woods for battered and quirky furniture: you want the feel to be eclectic and organic. Find picture frames and paint them in delphinium and pinked gray, which will look great hung against the deep blueberry walls.

Hunting *for truffles*

The velvety gray-brown of truffles sits perfectly with violets.

The most expensive edible fungi, truffles are found around the bases of oak and chestnut trees in the forests of France and Italy. They are revered for their taste and supposed aphrodisiac properties, and their color is inspirational to this scheme.

1

2

3

In a large drawing or sitting room, paint the main walls in iris (1). If the room has a wooden fireplace mantel, paint it natural stone (3), a color that sits beautifully against iris. If the fireplace needs replacing or creating, commission a simple design in real stone.

4

5

Carpet the floor in rich, velvety truffle (2), choosing a soft, deep-pile carpet that looks sumptuous and feels fabulous underfoot. Add upholstered furniture in a mix of lichen (4) and granite blue (5), and accessorize in iris and truffle.

Violet *surprise*

The word "violet" is commonly associated with the flower from which the name is derived. These flowers are a shade of purple that is a mixture of both blue and red and are the color basis for this violet scheme could be applied anywhere but works especially well in a kitchen.

Beautiful violets that translate well in a kitchen.

1

2

3

Use iris (1) as the main color for walls and play off this color with kitchen units painted in a mixture of violet white (2) and dark stone (3), using more of one color than the other so that the units don't look too even.
Use indigo (5) as a countertop color for the full run of the kitchen.

4

5

Finish with vibrant blue-violet (4) kitchen stools or chairs, which look funky and fun, and accessorize with cookware in either violet white or dark stone and beautiful dinnerware in any of these colors, or a combination of all of them.

By *the stream*

Where better to replicate water than the bathroom?

Water has many distinct properties. It is integral to the world and the proliferation of its life-forms. It has various religious symbolisms and is explored in many arts. Embracing the calming and reflective qualities of water in interiors is an important aspect of the ancient art of feng shui.

1

2

3

Simply by replicating the colors of water you can bring its calming, soothing benefits into your own environment.

Paint bluebell (1) on the walls and any tongue-and-groove paneling that you may have. Find a beautiful natural stone or travertine floor tile in blush stone (4) and clay (5); alternatively, paint floorboards in blush stone.

4

5

To finish the scheme, add towels and accessories in metallic blue (2) and Amazon blue (3).

Summer *fields*

Imagine yourself on a bright and sunny Sunday afternoon, meandering through the fields and absorbing the heady aromas of summertime. To bring the memories of this perfect time into your home, try implementing this scheme in your living room or a more formal lounge.

A selection of summertime colors perfect for a lounge.

1

2

3

Paint or paper walls in bluebell (1), and paint the inside fascia of a fireplace or a dresser or large piece of furniture in powder blue (4). Upholster sofas in apple white (2) and lake (5), using a striped fabric or one with a subtle pattern encompassing these two colors.

4

Dress windows in simple curtains in corn (3) edged along the bottom in lake if you wish. Pull all of these gentle colors together with accessories, cushions and objects d'art.

5

In *bloom*

A fresh, fragrant, floral delight to adorn a living room.

Both the color and beauty of flowers have always been an inspiration to artists and designers alike. The essence of flowers—their shape, texture and color—have been depicted throughout centuries, but it is difficult to capture their freshness and scent.

1

2

3

Capture these floral qualities by employing these colors in a domestic setting. Delicate cornflower (1) is a cool blue with gray undertones, suited to a lounge or living room.

4

A warm, natural oak floor would work well against cornflower walls. Alternatively, use natural burlap (3) as a carpet or floor covering. Use lily pink (2) for traditional upholstery, mixed with antique leather (5) for the odd chair or footstool.

5

Add curtains or shades in heavy woven fabrics in deep cornflower (4) and natural burlap.

Earth *tones*

This book features a number of schemes that draw upon nature and the world around us, and this group of colors is another that does so. For a relaxed and amiable scheme, tone these warm, earthy neutrals with the cooler, contrasting, limestonelike qualities of cornflower.

A scheme that reflects the natural earth around us.

1

2

3

Implement this scheme in an entrance hall for a stunning, contemporary look. Carpet the floor and the stairs in a cornflower (1) runner. Paint the staircase and above the chair rail in light sand (2), and use cornflower below it—this looks particularly striking if the walls are paneled.

4

5

Upholster window seats or occasional chairs in light tan (4) or soft, earth brown (5) leather. Complete the look with a selection of fabrics and accessories in khaki (3), cornflower and light sand.

Secret *garden*

*Fall in love instantly
with this dreamy
bouquet of colors.*

Flowers provide enjoyment for many, whether in the neat
colorful beds of the garden, growing wild in fields or meadows
or carefully arranged in vases. Like the heady scent of freshly
picked flowers, these gorgeous
floral-inspired colors will work
well in a bedroom.

1

2

3

Paint or paper the walls in
hyacinth (1) and carpet in the
same hue, giving the room a
dreamlike quality, all fluffy and
feminine. If you want to include
a feature wall, look for hyacinth
wallpaper with hints
of green stone (2) and
darker bark green (5).

4

5

Go ultra girly and
curtain in rose (3) and
hyacinth in a delicate
floral fabric, or go
more neutral with bark
green (5) and gooseberry (4).
Upholstery should tie in with the
choice of curtaining, but if you
have chosen a fussy curtain fabric,
use a simple single shade for
upholstery, and vice versa.

Sweet *dreams*

Continuing with the soft, fragrant, delicate qualities of flowers, consider the silky-soft texture of a rose petal, how sensual it is to touch, and try to recreate that feel with tactile fabrics. The softness and femininity of this scheme makes it ideal for a girly bedroom.

A floral scheme perfect for a little girl's bedroom.

1

2

3

Paint the walls in hyacinth (1), reserving one wall or a chimney breast for a simple mural of hearts or dots and stars in lilac (2), rich cream (3) and hyacinth—you could even embellish the mural with stick-on crystals and buttons.

4

Carpet the room in fudge (4) or, as a lighter alternative, paint floorboards in rich cream.

5

Paint furniture in rich cream, with fun colored handles in lilac. Choose simple cotton bedding in latte (5) and fudge (4), with pretty dress pillows in lilac and hyacinth.

Changing *seasons*

A palette driven by the changing colors of fall.

As leaves change color through the year, trees and foliage can offer an infinite number of color permutations and combinations to draw upon. Combine the warmth of the fall colors with cooler gray tones for a beautiful lounge or living area.

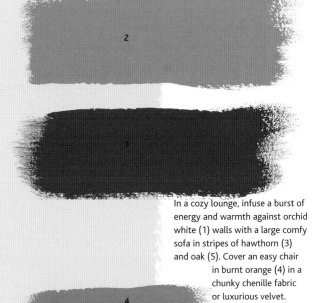

In a cozy lounge, infuse a burst of energy and warmth against orchid white (1) walls with a large comfy sofa in stripes of hawthorn (3) and oak (5). Cover an easy chair in burnt orange (4) in a chunky chenille fabric or luxurious velvet.

Select a natural floor covering or carpet in wood smoke (2), and make sure you add plenty of artwork and a selection of accessories, taking the boldness of hawthorn through the room.

Grand, *elegant Victorian charm*

Victorian colors are generally thought of as dark, muted tones, but they do work wonderfully well in large, formal settings. Team neutrals with deep, rich accents for a traditional feel and to inject a sense of grandeur into a formal lounge, dining or drawing room.

Rich, classic colors for traditional splendor.

1

2

3

Paint walls in Regency green (2), punctuating this deep, classical color with a chair rail, picture rail, cornice and all woodwork finished in orchid white (1).

Contrast orchid white floorboards with deep, rich walnut (5) furniture. Upholster dining chair seat pads or full chairs or sofas in gorgeous biscuit (4) velvet.

4

5

Place tall glass lamps with huge silk shades in rose peach (3) on a sideboard or console table to finish.

Return to nature

Immerse yourself in healing green. Calming,
energizing and stimulating, greens are an ideal way
to bring the outside into our homes. This chapter
focuses on those colors found naturally in the
landscapes around us. Simply look outside your
window. Be inspired and ignited by what surrounds
you; falling leaves of autumnal neutrals against hints
of silver birch, secret clearings deep in the forest,
placid lakes and still skies.

Lush *mangroves*

*Blend the garden
room and garden.*

The colors of nature are an amazing source of inspiration from which we should take reference. In this palette, green, the color of life and growth, is the primary focus, and will help you bring the freshness of the outside in. Use this scheme to extend the outdoors into a sunroom or summerhouse.

Paint the walls within the sunroom or summerhouse in tranquil buff (3), and mirror this outside by painting an external wall in the same color.

Reflect the greens in the vegetation outside by using seaweed (1) for sunroom furniture, with shades of foliage (4) and green earth (5) in loose cushions.

Finally, take praline (2) wood flooring through the sunroom and outside to a decked patio to create the perfect environment for a glass of wine with friends.

Summer *meadows*

When an area of grassland is left uncultivated, the very ordinary but beautiful flowers and plants that punctuate the expanse of green are simply breathtaking. Irregular patterns, varying colors, and heavenly scents all make for perfect inspiration.

Create an eclectic mix of meadow colors for a traditional bedroom.

1

2

3

To recreate this summer mix in a bedroom, paint a seaweed (1) feature wall behind a traditional wrought-iron bed. Paint some shaker-style bedside tables in alpine white (2), and use the same color on the remaining walls for a striking contrast to the dark seaweed.

4

5

Buy colorful patchwork quilts and comforters in mulberry (5), dusky mauve (4) and grass (3), and a selection of plain cushions covered in any one of these accent colors. To finish, place pretty vases of wildflowers on the bedside table.

Nature's *finery*

For a formal dining room keep things ordered and symmetrical.

This palette makes use of the hues of nature's woodland. The deep greens and rich browns shown here are ideal for a formal setting—either a dining or formal reception room. To make an impression, you need good-quality furniture and fabrics, as well as a refined approach to decoration.

Lighting is an essential part of a good dining experience: you don't want to be blinded, but at the same time you would like to see what you are eating.

Paint the walls in rich sage green (1) and add pairs of contemporary wall lights with conker (3) wood bases and yellow-cream (4) shades. Keep furniture to a minimum, just a large table and a sideboard in conker-colored wood, and upholster chairs in simple but elegant warm stone (5). Curtain with floor-length drapes in putty (2).

Unexplored *landscape*

It is relatively easy to decorate large rooms. In smaller spaces, you need to think carefully about colors and maximizing space. Choose quiet grays and blue-greens for a snug or home office, remembering that in small spaces it's important to keep clutter hidden and ensure that what is on display is attractive and neat.

In small spaces work up schemes with gentle hues.

1

2

3

Use sage green (1) as the main focal color of the room, and upholster any chairs or freestanding furniture in this shade. Set this furniture against winter white (4) walls and a moon blue (2) carpet. To keep it looking streamlined, light and airy, paint shelving winter white as well.

4

At the window, fit wooden shutters or a simple roller blind in verdigris (3). Use warm gray (5) and sage green as the colors for any storage, such as box files, folders and containers.

5

Silver *birch*

Cool, sophisticated colors for a classic drawing room.

Using a cool, calm, and collected palette, lift ash gray perfectly by adding icy blue and dove gray, before combining these with further green accents. These beautiful, timeless colors are suited to both period and contemporary settings.

1

2

3

This scheme can work in any kind of room if used thoughtfully. For a dramatic effect use ash gray (1) and meadow green (5) as your main wall colors. For a more subtle scheme, use barely there icy blue (2) and dove gray (3). Dove gray will also make a fabulous carpet or floor color in this scheme.

4

5

Re-cover an old chair or sofa in deep moss (4) velvet for a rich, luxurious finish. Use the remaining colors for cushions, curtains and other accents.

Sun-drenched *orchard*

Imagine the sun soaking an apple orchard or flooding a citrus grove or a large, woven basket filled with the ripened fruits collected from this forest garden. This palette takes reference from this rural scene and is the perfect kitchen scheme for a rambling farmhouse or converted barn.

A fresh, fruity scheme inspired by rural living.

1

2

3

For the centerpiece of a family country kitchen, nothing beats a gorgeous vintage stove; choose pale apple (2) if you can.

Paint the walls of your chosen room with ash gray (1), and find some beautiful backsplash tiles in shades of ash gray and mint white (3).

4

Mix kitchen units in warm oak with golden (4) and straw (5) hand-painted cupboards for a rustic, country look. Accessorize with similar rustic-style cookware.

5

Shimmering *light*

Unusual dark colors paired with flashes of bright highlights.

The effect of light upon water is the main inspiration for this dramatic palette. Freshen up a canal green base with a combination of both light and dark accents for a lavish vintage bedroom in true 1930s-style glamour.

1

2

3

4

5

Use classic glass table lamps and geometric mirrors to throw light around canal green (1) walls. Upholster an oversized headboard in raspberry (4) silk, buttoned and edged with bitter chocolate (5), and add wall lights either side of the bed in bitter chocolate.

Place a chaise longue under a window, upholstered in a devoré print of raspberry and acorn (3), with bitter chocolate feet.

Carpet the room in ivory (2) to balance the dark colors, and accessorize with Deco sculptures.

Evoking *twilight*

The unusual ambient light of twilight has long been popular with painters and photographers, who refer to it as the "blue hour," after the French expression *l'heure bleue*. As night draws in, these twilight colors will create an escape from the traumas of the working day.

Mysterious and soothing muted colors evoke a calming ambience.

1

2

3

Use dusk sky (2) as an evocative neutral for a feature wall; its hints of gray and pink make for a mysterious tone. Bring canal green (1) in for the remaining walls, and curtain in a lighter shade of this color with hints of deep teal (4).

4

Stain a wooden floor in rich nutmeg (3); all the better if the wood is a little battered and not too perfect.

5

Upholster elegant and comfortable sofas in canal green, and fluff up with extra cushions in spearmint (5) and deep teal. Light the fire and numerous candles and begin to unwind.

Natural *stone*

Warm tonal greens and creams ideal for a child's bedroom.

Wild and garish colors are not always desired for a child's room—it can be far more restful to create an inviting, calming space. However, children's rooms should be interesting and fun, with plenty of storage and decoration to inspire.

1

2

3

Use warm stone (1) as your wall color and sand (2) as the hue for a hard-wearing but soft carpet. Into an alcove add painted shelves in pale yellow (3).

Fill the shelves with books, and glue rows of shells, chestnuts and acorns in box frames to create natural artworks that look stylish and smart.

4

5

Use pale yellow for bedroom furniture with foliage (4) handles, and add a fun striped or checked rug in lake (5) and pale yellow to complete this stylish child's bedroom.

Past *antiquities*

If you have collected pieces of furniture or artifacts from travels, it's always nice to be able to display them but in a relaxed way; you don't want to feel like you're living in a museum! The trick is to group items of similar color or type and keep the decor in the room pared down and neutral.

A scheme that will evolve beautifully over time.

1

2

3

Warm stone (1) is a great warm neutral that can be used as a backdrop in any room. Use this shade to cover your walls.

Rose lip (2) is an unusual tone but gives a fresh look for upholstery fabric on old wing chairs. It also works especially well with muted orange (3), a classic color for drapes.

4

5

Use warm stone, avocado (4) and blackish-green (5) as colors for further upholstery. Finish with accessories in any of these colors or a combination of all of them.

Autumnal *richness*

Bring the rich, warm colors of fall into a dining room.

The ochers and varying browns of fall leaves are the inspiration behind this palette. These seasonal, rich tones are perfect for a warm and homely dining room scheme but will also work equally well in a cozy lounge or living area.

1

2

3

4

5

For your base, paint the walls of your chosen room in natural limestone (1), and make a feature of the wall opposite the main window by painting it poppy (5).

Place a console table in cocoa bean (3) against the poppy wall, and add a pair of lamps with cinnamon (2) shades. Mirror this on the dining table with a finish in cocoa bean, and a table runner that combines khaki green (4) and cinnamon.

Upholster chairs in cinnamon to complete the ensemble.

Crisp, *fresh and inviting*

Snow-covered landscapes, steely winter skies and snowdrops peeking through the spring ground; be inspired by the cool, calming time of year when hope is restored and we look forward to the warmth of summer.

Crisp, relaxed colors for an entrance that welcomes visitors.

1

2

3

Tile the floor that leads off into a kitchen or dining room in natural limestone (1).

Panel the hall and paint the paneling in limestone also, so it seamlessly flows from one application to another. Paint the wall above in misted pink (2).

4

Add a pair of ceramic umbrella stands or decorative floor vases in icicle (3), pinked taupe (4) or apple cream (5) to frame the start of the hall and make for an inviting finish.

5

Woodland *fell*

Use the subtle shades of nature in a bedroom.

You might come upon these shades on a nature ramble, but their quiet beauty is equally at home in a modern apartment. A resourceful color, brown stone mixed with the calming shade of marble is ideal for sleeping spaces.

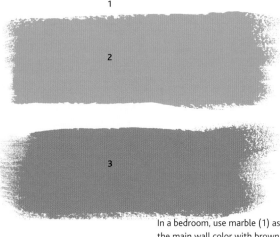

In a bedroom, use marble (1) as the main wall color with brown stone (2) painted bedside tables and furniture. Khaki green (3), petal (4) or tobacco (5) would make a fabulous headboard in a textured linen fabric or raw silk and look great against fresh bed linen in petal. Adorn the bed with plump cushions in the same shade chosen for the headboard.

This scheme also works well in a modern open-plan kitchen/living space. In a kitchen, try the work surfaces in tobacco, and paint units in petal and brown stone.

Misty *morning*

This scheme was inspired by a brisk stroll in the early morning. As the sunlight begins to burn through the mist, the landscape becomes clear and refined. Implement this light, fresh scheme in an interior for a graceful, elegant living space.

Layer warm and cool neutrals for a stylish living room.

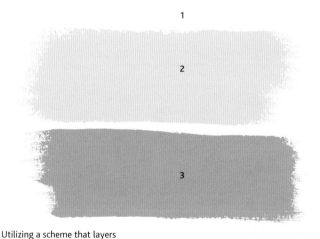

1

2

3

Utilizing a scheme that layers both warm and cool neutrals in a room will help you transcend light and dark. Use ambiguous marble (1) as a cheery base neutral for your living area, and couple with the darkest accent in the group—flagstone gray (3)—as flooring. Add contemporary sofas upholstered in taupe (2) leather, and place large floor cushions in bluebell gray (5) around a central coffee table.

4

5

Use rain cloud (4) to create your own full-length drapes that hang simply and make a feature of the windows, and accessorize with any of these accent shades.

Bracken, *moss and ferns*

Promote relaxation with a range of leafy tones.

Green is synonymous with nature and energy. It's calming, restful and balanced, so anywhere you want to relax will benefit from an injection of this color. If you have a large bathroom make the most of these relaxing tones to create a perfect hideaway.

1

2

3

4

5

Use bath stone (1) as the color for both wall and floor tiles. Paint any remaining wall space in foliage (2), and use deep forest (5) and the other green tones for plump towels and bathroom accessories.

Paint the exterior of a claw-foot tub in soft wood (3), and keep the fixtures in clean, fresh pure white (4).

A natural oak would also work with these tones, so if you have space for freestanding furniture you may consider bringing in this finish.

Lost *in the forest*

Enter a forest and you begin a magical journey through whispering trees and unknown territories—a feeling that you can replicate at home. Find a beautiful, subtle floral-inspired wallpaper that brings together bath stone and pebble gray, and use it to paper the whole room or just one wall.

Replicate the mysteries of a deep, tree-lined forest in a bedroom.

With your walls ready, carpet the room or paint floorboards in warm bath stone (1). Pick a plain woven fabric in field green (3) for window dressings; Roman blinds in this shade edged with pebble gray (4) and with natural leather pulls will look fabulous.

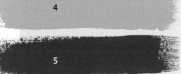

Choose a contemporary deep serpentine (5) four-poster bed with simple lines as a focal point of the room. At the foot of the bed, upholster a footstool or bench in vibrant jade (2) for a flash of strong color.

Beauty
of the desert

Warming and enlivening, the sunshine tones of yellows
will inject soul into any interior space. From pared-
down yellow-creams to pigment-rich golden saffrons,
use yellows as a base to brighten and lighten cooler
north-facing spaces. Take inspiration from the midday
heat of the Kalahari Desert—its space and clay-baked
landscape. Imagine dried-out grasses strewn across an
expanse of golden sand and the hot sun scorching the
earth beneath, and implement the warmth of browns,
yellows and oranges at home.

Lost *oasis*

A bright, fun and energizing scheme fit for a bedroom.

Reminiscent of the hot, dry desert, the warm ochers of this palette work especially well with contrasting cool accents. While the almost tropical tones are lively and energizing, the cool blue components of the group will give a calmer edge to the scheme, perfect for an older child's bedroom or study.

1

2

3

4

5

In your chosen room, paint walls in bright sunflower (1) for a bright, bold backdrop.

Choose the lightest color, desert cream (4), as a carpet or painted floor. If you decide to paint the floor, add funky rugs in pool (2), azure (3), sunflower and rich golden (5).

For curtains, choose a stylized floral or patterned print that brings all of these colors together, and frame pop-art-style prints in white box frames and hang them in sets on the walls to finish the look.

Bazaar *style*

Imagine the old bazaar in Cairo; busy, bustling, noisy streets lined with colorful stalls selling cloth, clothing, spices, foodstuffs, traditional jewelry and souvenirs. For understated elegance take inspiration from the tactile qualities of these items, particularly the fabrics.

Take inspiration from the colors of an Egyptian bazaar.

1

2

3

Be adventurous and upholster a modern L-shaped sofa in bright sunflower (1). Against a neutral backdrop of natural (2) and gray sand (3), a velvet, chenille, or leather sofa in this shade will look like a real designer statement.

4

5

Accentuate the boldness of the sofa choice with beautiful cushions in cooler blackcurrant (4) and golden brown (5), using patterns and embroidered pieces as well as plains. To complete the look, add authentic pieces in any of these colors.

Nomadic *charm*

Unique and luxurious, combine unusual colors with dark woods.

This scheme has only two basic colors, but by playing with the shades and their applications you can ensure the room feels rich and luxurious. Combine this palette with dark wood, mirrored finishes and good-quality furniture for a deluxe and stunning overall effect.

1

2

3

The centerpiece of the room could be a huge yellow-ocher (1) drum-pendant light shade, which will look amazing against matte dusky mauve (3) walls.

4

5

Use a sumptuous eggplant (5) velvet for the sofa and yellow ocher and India yellow (4) silk for cushions to really intensify the injection of yellow in the scheme.

Find a textured, silky large rug in mushroom (2) for the center of the room, and finish with ornate mirrors and gilt frames on the walls.

Scorched *earth*

Light, bright or cool colors are the stereotypical colors for a bathroom—cool blues, grays or whites, for example—and so you might not think this is a suitable palette for such a room. But if you have a reasonably sized room and the space to accommodate a freestanding tub it's perfect.

A warm but relaxed and gentle scheme fit for a bathroom.

1

2

3

Paint the walls in yellow ocher (1) and the external face of the tub in dark stone (3).

Use burlap (2) as a floor color and find colonial pieces of freestanding furniture and accessories in dark wood to contrast with the floor.

4

For the window, make a simple shade in yellow ocher edged with dark stone, and use mirrors to maximize the light.

5

Finally, choose a selection of plain and striped towels in pot pink (4), terra-cotta (5) and burlap.

Spice *market*

An opulent set of spicy colors, perfect for a dining room.

The spice trade developed in the Middle East in around 2000 BCE, and in the Middle Ages spices were among the most luxurious products available in Europe. Their aromatic flavorings are the inspiration for these rich tones, which combine to create a chic, elegant scheme.

1

2

3

Find antique furniture in rich mahogany (2) and reupholster the chairs in golden saffron (1). Replicate golden saffron, but not necessarily in the same fabric, in full-length curtains to enhance the ceiling height. Paint the walls in elephant (4); the yellow tones of saffron look fabulous next to matte gray paint.

4

5

Lighting is crucial to setting the right ambiance in a dining room, so pair lamps on a sideboard or console table with oversized shades in jet (5), and in a corner place a standard lamp with a similarly shaped shade in burlap (3).

Windswept *dunes*

Picture an open expanse of golden sand dunes, unspoiled and seemingly endless, falling softly against the surrounding coastal landscape from which the dunes are forged. Use these colors to create your very own indoor paradise, an ideal respite from the demands of daily life.

Warm a pastel scheme with soft textures and dark wood.

1

2

3

In a lounge, choose a dramatic wallpaper in golden saffron (1) and lily (2) to act as a backdrop to gray-lilac (3) upholstered furniture. Add woven throws and woolen cushions in gray-lilac, gold tint (4) and clay (5).

Carpet the sitting area in clay (5), or, if you have a wood floor, use a large textured rug to define a cozy area.

4

5

To complete, find a complementary fabric that brings lily and gray-lilac tones and golden saffron together, and hang simple curtains from a luxurious, chunky dark-wood pole.

Mexican *hot*

*A sizzling scheme
ideal for a modern
living space.*

Fiery, hot and spicy, the Mexican influence in this scheme
is energizing, outgoing and above all, fun. Mix orange and
brown with the warm tones
of buttermilk for a scheme
that would work well in a
modern lounge or open-plan
living area.

1

2

3

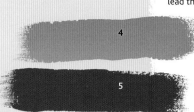

4

5

Paint two adjoining walls in rich
buttermilk (1) and the rest with
an inoffensive neutral such as
beige linen (3), which will allow
the yellow to be the star and
lead the eye into the area you've
chosen to define.

Use pure white (2)
for the woodwork.
Find a good retro fabric
for window shades in
rich buttermilk and
hot orange (4).

Pick out key accessories
in hot orange, perhaps
a funky chair in the corner or a
fabulous lamp, and finish with
dark wood (5) contemporary
furniture in simple, clean shapes.

Pared-down *living*

Cheery, bright and refreshing, yellow is the color associated with sunshine and light. Yellow works particularly well with greens and oranges and can be either brightened or subdued, depending on the accents it is teamed with. Seen as welcoming and upbeat, it is the perfect shade for a kitchen or hallway.

Use yellow to bring a little sunshine into the room.

1

2

3

4

5

What better place to employ the attributes of rich buttermilk (1) than on the walls of an entrance hall, where you welcome guests into your home?

Keep the woodwork in clean white (3), which works extremely well with all yellows. Choose a woven runner in sage (2), yellowed cream (4), and gold ocher (5), remembering that stripes are particularly smart for hall and stair runners.

Add some greenery in gold ocher and yellowed cream pots on the window ledges or furniture tops to complete the look.

Californian *cactus*

For a modern palette opt for zesty yellows and lime greens.

This scheme combines the warm, arid color of sandstone with fragrant citrus accents. The subtlety of warm sandstone is complemented perfectly by these sharp, refreshing shades, resulting in a bold scheme, ideal for a contemporary kitchen.

1

2

3

Warm sandstone (1) has delicate cream-yellow tones that make it ideal for a painted kitchen, but keep the overall feeling light with countertops, handles and tiling in cream (3).

4

For a bright, refreshing wake-up call in the morning, include flashes of color in lime green (5).

5

Paint an old kitchen table in honey (2), leaving the top in wood or painted cream, and paint a few odd chairs in a slightly paler lime green (4).

Complete the look with colorful zesty accessories and, of course, a few funky cacti in pots.

Desert *rose*

Warm yellows sit easily next to each other, and their warmth makes them perfect for a room that is naturally very cool or doesn't get much natural light. Yellow is a good reflector of sunlight, so it will make a dark room appear lighter and brighter.

A glorious range of yellows to emit light and warmth.

1

2

3

Implement this glowing, golden scheme and bring artificial sunshine into any room.

In a lounge, paint the walls in warm sandstone (1) and carpet in contrasting rich gold ocher (5). Upholster furniture in a stripe fabric of beach yellow (2) and vanilla fudge (3), adding beautiful woven cushions in hues of pale orange (4) and gold ocher.

4

5

When dressing windows, remember to keep curtains bright and light, making sure they don't block out the natural daylight.

Calming *classics*

A thoroughly modern look with a crisp, classic edge.

White— crisp, clean and fresh—is often seen as a clinical color, but it works particularly well with yellow. This palette really capitalizes on the harmonious relationship of these two hues, creating a scheme that works especially well in a family kitchen.

1

2

3

4

5

For a minimal but classic country kitchen, try painting all cupboards and woodwork in pure white (2), and finish with timeless brass handles. Include matching taps in brass also. Use pure white and metallic gray (5) as the colors for a sleek marble countertop.

For a sunny backdrop, paint the walls in pale gold (1). The warm tones of this shade will contrast nicely with the cooler tones of the marble.

Pick out pieces of ceramic, storage jars and dinnerware in warm clay (3), banana (4) and metallic gray to finish.

Interior *paradise*

Certain colors evoke different feelings or moods. You can instantly create a mood by changing the color of a room. Where you want to feel relaxed and comfortable stick to a good base of warm neutrals that can be taken as a staple through to other rooms.

The simplest way to update your home is with color.

1

2

3

When working with a warm yellow neutral such as pale gold (1), use beige tones like natural stone (2) and dark stone (3) to complement it, perhaps as a carpet that runs through from the lounge to the hall, tying the rooms together.

4

To add depth and a flash of color pick out prints and woven fabrics in midnight (4) and natural stone, which will look great next to pale gold.

5

For a contemporary twist to the scheme, include pieces of furniture in herb (5) and shiny chrome to give the relaxed scheme some glamour.

Arabian *nights*

Combine earthly colors and bold prints in an exotic den.

The colors and trends of the Arabian way of life are the inspiration behind this scheme: bold prints, sumptuous drapery and ambient lighting effects against a beautiful scenic backdrop. For your interior, pull influence from Arabic styling but don't make it look like a stage set.

1

2

3

A base color of sand dune (1) allows you to be really creative with colors and patterns. Complement sand dune walls with other earthy neutrals such as natural stone (2) and green clay (3). This unobtrusive backdrop can be accentuated with flashes of strong color; use gamboge (4) and copper rust (5) in a large striped rug in the center of the room or as the colors for a block-printed throw or window shade.

4

5

Accessorize with candles and lanterns fitting to the theme.

Bedouin *silks*

Staying with the Arabian theme, this scheme takes reference from the nomadic desert tribe of the Bedouin. Evoke the exotic feel of a Bedouin tent with layered throws, woven cloths with metallic threads and bolster cushions strewn across a large dark-wood bed.

Natural silks and velvets for a plush feel to the bedroom.

Like the desert surrounding the tent, paint the walls in sand dune (1), and as a centerpiece find a decadent red mahogany (3) bed.

Scour specialist stores for unusual cushions in purple (4) and deepest peacock (5) embellished with shiny details in metallic pink (2). Use offcuts of velvets and silks to make more cushions and throws.

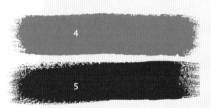

Choose a woven burlap flooring in sand dune or a shade darker to give a neutral backdrop to the tactile fabrics around the room.

Moving *landscape*

Similarly toned colors for a flawless interior scheme.

Natural light has a dramatic effect on the landscape, from the crisp white light of the morning to the moody softness of dusk. Artificial light has a similar effect, and this must be taken into account when selecting an interior color scheme.

1

2

3

Colors respond to light, so when choosing a color paint a small test area first and observe throughout the day and at night; you may find it looks completely different at certain times.

4

Desert cream (1) is a perfect neutral to base the scheme around. Use old white (4) for woodwork and pick a floor covering in desert cream.

5

In a lounge, use combinations of pastel lemon (2), celadon (3) and light teal (5) for upholstery and soft furnishings, and curtain with simple voiles in old white to make the best of the natural light.

Limitless *ground*

The taupe family is extensive, and this scheme takes its color inspiration from those shades and the natural world around us. Team these natural shades with a range of materials and textures for a stunning, truly decadent bedroom.

Add natural materials to a neutral scheme for timeless elegance.

For a boutique bedroom, paint walls in desert cream (1), and curtain in weighty, full-length drapes in a textured taupe-green (2) fabric.

Choose good-quality cotton bedding in either pure white or a mix of desert cream and sand taupe (3).

Furniture should be dark in contrast, either almost black or walnut. Upholster a bedroom stool or statement chair in yellow-cream (4), and place a fabulous moleskin (5) velvet cushion on the seat. Add cushions in the same shade to the bed.

Moroccan dreams

Picture mud hut villages nestled in a sun-soaked landscape, clear skies, rolling mountains scattered with delicate flowers and lost worlds dotted with Bedouin tents and colorful textiles. This chapter takes inspiration from the Moroccan way of life and uses a range of earth oranges to harmonize and warm a number of different interior spaces.

Thé *à la menthe*

This mix of exotic colors would suit a bedroom or lounge.

In Morocco, drinking tea with family and friends is an important ritual. The locals drink incredibly sweet mint tea from beautiful shot-type glasses that are often gilded or colored—a delicious color combination that is the inspiration for this scheme.

1

2

3

4

5

Use dark spice (1) as a stain for a wood floor, and soften it with rugs in stripes of Moroccan pink (2), white sand (3), milk white (4) and Thai green (5).

Add bolster cushions and woven throws over plain seating or beds, and paint furniture in milk white and dark spice.

Pick up on the striking green accents by accessorizing with pretty glass tea-light holders or vases in Thai green.

Ancient *origins*

These orange neutrals are reminiscent of the desert and the subtle color changes it can produce. An image springs to mind of a Berber village that appears from nowhere through the dunes. Let these colors take you back in time and transport you to an ancient world.

A warm, smart scheme to capture the mystical allure of Morocco.

1

2

3

This versatile scheme will work throughout the house. Use these tones in an open-plan space, defining the living areas with walls in dark spice (1) and taking taupe-cream (2) through the kitchen and dining area. Bring the dark spice back into the kitchen with high-gloss units.

4

For uniformity, use straight shades or blinds throughout in ash brown (3), and for seating, choose contemporary sofas in Naples yellow (4) and a single chair in golden umber (5).

5

Natural *pigments*

Use these basic tones in a contemplative study or home office.

In the past, pigments were made by grinding minerals and plants, which meant that colors were limited and some very expensive to produce. Today, pigments are made from chemicals, resulting in a kaleidoscope of colors, but this scheme is inspired by the earlier varieties.

Go back to the very roots of colors; use Berber brown (1) and deep amber (3) as a striped or checked carpet, and paint the walls in cinnamon peach (2). Make simple shades for the windows in Berber brown.

Use mineral (4) for an industrial-style desk, complemented by a steel blue (5) chair.

To finish, frame a range of sepia images in mineral frames and hang in sets on the walls.

Moorish *charm*

The intense decoration and workmanship of existing Moorish architecture is an incredible site to behold. One of the most impressive examples is the Alhambra in Granada, Spain, which hides many surprises in its infinite palaces and palatial gardens and is the inspiration for this color palette.

The perfect scheme for a retro-styled interior.

The surprise in this scheme is the injection of fiery hot orange (5), which works fabulously as an accent in a retro lounge.

Choose stylish low leather sofas in Berber brown (1), and keep the walls in the background discreet by painting them with ivory (2).

Use nude (3) for a carpet, and in the center of the room place a huge rug featuring tones of pot pink (4) and hot orange.

Finish with a quirky arc lamp with a hot orange shade.

Chasing *gold*

Golden tones add warmth to a dull room or apartment.

Gold has been highly valued since prehistoric times. Associated with wealth, riches, coinage and jewelry, gold readily forms alloys with many other metals, and in a similar way it bonds well with many other hues. Various tones of gold work beautifully well with the browns selected here.

1

2

3

Use peach butter (3) in a carpet that runs through the whole ground floor. Paint all wall space in raw sienna (1).

Pick clean-lined pieces of furniture—retro and new—in mahogany (5), which will look great next to the raw sienna walls and peach butter carpet. Upholster a main piece of furniture in yellowed gold (2), use this as your focal point and accessorize with shades of milk chocolate (4).

4

5

For a contemporary twist, add modern prints or mirrors in gold frames.

159

Earthy *imagination*

Orange is a creative color that is bursting with energy. Its spectrum is huge, from fiery blood oranges to the deep chestnut browns of the earth. As with many other colors, the appearance of this shade will be influenced by the colors it is grouped with. When placed with calmer neutrals, raw sienna will appear as a rich orange.

Energetic shades to create a flexible and fun environment.

1

2

3

Implement this scheme in a teenager's lounge or children's playroom.

Use raw sienna (1) as your base color on the walls. Flooring would work in chocolate caramel (3), and woodwork or any permanent details in the lighter calico (2).

4

For seating use chalk cream (4), and accessorize with Roman clay (5) and raw sienna cushions and beanbags. Similarly, use these shades for bedding and accompanying cushions for a bedroom setting.

5

House *of green mint*

*Bring the heat
of Morocco into
your bedroom.*

Evoke the feel of a Moroccan villa hidden within the lush foliage of a hot, arid landscape surrounded by fountains and trickling water that cool and calm the senses in the hot desert sun. This is the perfect paradise to recreate in a bedroom.

1

2

3

4

5

Paint the walls of your bedroom in spicy amber (1), letting the warm glow envelop the room. Add painted furniture in the contrasting silver-white (2) and a beautiful silk headboard in flagstone gray (3).

Hang flowing lengths of luxurious spicy amber and menthe (5) sheers at the windows and a deep green leaf (4) shade inside for practical privacy.

Crisp, fresh bed linen in silver-white will make for an inviting bed, which can be accessorized with cushions in any one or a combination of these shades.

Arabic *exoticism*

When echoing a period or a culture in home decoration, take elements of the theme rather than a picture-book copy. Play with scales and contrast to make something ordinary into something unique. For instance, put large floor lamps either side of a bed instead of nightstands and bedside lamps.

Calm neutrals to accentuate spicy Arabian shades.

Use spicy amber (1) as the color for two large Arabic urns either side of a pinked gray (2) colored fireplace. Paint the walls in soothing lavender water (3), and cover the floor in natural stone (4).

A spicy warm gold (5) will make a gorgeous sofa tone; keep it low and against the wall like banquette seating, and cover in cushions of various textures that echo all of these selected colors.

Finally, treat windows by dressing them in curtains or shades in pinked gray.

Foreign *spices*

Bring the flavors of Africa into your kitchen.

When you visit a North African country, the abundance of spices is awe inspiring. The flavors and colors of the cuisine are mouthwatering, and the taste sensation leaves you wanting more. Use this scheme to incorporate these foreign flavors into your home.

1

2

3

Use Moorish orange (1) to clad your kitchen walls in spice. With such a strong color on the walls it's a good idea to keep the kitchen itself plain, with units in soft butter cream (4). Contrast these light kitchen units with a glorious dark green-brown (3) floor.

4

5

Tagine orange (2) would make a great surprise color for trendy leather breakfast stools, while calmer pale butternut (5) shades would punctuate the Moorish orange walls. Include cookware in tagine orange and green-brown tones.

Mysterious *Marrakech*

To instill mystery in a design you need to add elements
that people want to know more about or things they don't
understand or expect. To do this with an interior, use old pieces
of furniture, quirky antique objects and interesting artworks,
or even try using old trunks as
coffee tables.

*Unusual objects and
unique furniture for
a touch of mystery.*

Use Moorish orange (1) as a focal
point for a huge abstract painting
that almost fills a wall. Paint
the walls themselves in duck
egg (4)—this will contrast
beautifully with the painting.

Find retro black (5) sofas
that are sculptural and
smart, and for side
tables use an old hatbox
or perhaps a set of small
wooden steps.

For curtaining and
accessories use a
combination of rust rose (3)
and orange-cream (2) in varying
textures and finishes.

Moorish *romance*

A mix of sensual colors and fabrics for the bedroom.

For a seductive, oriental space, step straight out of a Moroccan souk and create a romantic terra-cotta and sand bedroom or snug. To accentuate the sensual environment, be sure to make the most of a range of plush, sexy fabrics.

1

2

3

As your backdrop, paint walls in sandstorm (1) and combine with billowing voiles in glorious yellow-cream (2).

Use over-the-top exotic decoration with a huge buttoned headboard in luxurious dark taupe (3) silk, with a bed covered in silk cushions in nude (4) and Roman pink (5).

4

5

Hang Moroccan jeweled star lanterns either side of the bed for romantic bedside lights that will project the geometric shapes when turned on.

Mediterranean *color*

In the arid desert landscape, beautiful Moroccan interiors are filled with explosions of color. A popular color is blue, and often a single feature, such as a door or table, is painted in this color, which resonates in and contrasts with the yellowed oranges and pinks that Morocco is so famous for.

Bold, playful colors perfect for children.

1

2

3

In a playroom, replicate this beautiful sunny Med blue (2) with a painted or high-gloss storage cupboard in which you can throw all the toys and games. Surround the cupboard with a wall painted sandstorm (1).

Add footstools and beanbags in Naples red (3) and Med blue as multifunctional seating. Keep the woodwork and ceilings in off-white (4).

4

5

For a bit of fun and interaction, paint a reachable area of wall space in blackboard (5) paint so the children can draw on the wall.

Sunset *at Essaouira*

A scheme to evoke the warmth of traditional Morocco.

The ancient city of Essaouira, peacefully nestled on the Atlantic coast, is a popular tourist destination in Morocco. The city has many boutique hotels created from Moroccan "riads," traditional dwellings centered around a courtyard and reminiscent of Roman villas.

1

2

3

The rich, warm colors of this scheme take inspiration from these traditional Moroccan communities. In a kitchen with a living or dining area extending to the yard, paint the kitchen area in Sahara sand (1) and the rest of the space in paler gray light (2). Use a natural stone (3) flooring throughout to tie the two spaces together.

4

5

Keep a bare deep brick (5) wall as a feature in a farmhouse-style kitchen, and accessorize with vases and planters in warm pink blush (4) and Sahara sand.

Mosaic *dream*

As a largely practical room, sometimes the bathroom doesn't get as much attention as other rooms in the home. Moroccan bathrooms, however, are both practical and luxurious, using muted sandstones, plaster-wash walls and subdued lighting. Take inspiration from this and treat your bathroom to a Moroccan makeover.

Bring your bathroom to life with bold colors and mosaics.

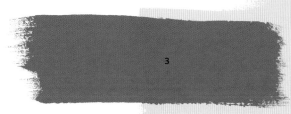

1

2

3

Arch a pillared opening onto a sunken tub and paint the back wall in the darkest color, cedar (3). For the face of the arch and the rest of the room, paint a light wash of Sahara sand (1) over white (2). This will ensure the room remains light and airy.

4

5

For the shower, create a wet-room area with a simple glass screen, then find some beautiful handmade mosaic tiles in violet wash (4) and oxide green (5). Add some glass and antique brass wall lanterns either side of a large mirror edged in the mosaics.

Desert *storm*

A combination of exotic desert hues and serene neutrals.

Desert storms can be fierce, violent and noisy, but they are often preceded and succeeded by a period of calm. To create a tranquil, secret escape from the hustle and bustle of everyday life, employ this color scheme in a living area and hint simply at a few chosen items from Moroccan life.

1

2

3

Use a pale palette of neutral colors and only the finest natural materials. Fill your lounge with an L-shaped sofa in butternut (1), as large as the room will allow. Paint walls in white sand (3) and carpet in a plush pale taupe (2). Place large floor cushions around and against the sofa in Saharan gold (4) and rust rose (5), and try not to add too much more furniture.

4

5

Curtain in butternut raw silk that billows on the floor, and hang on wrought-iron poles. Finish by adding abstract images on large canvases in sandy tones.

Concealed *paradise*

Wander around the mysterious streets of Marrakech and you would never know the beauty that lies beyond the high walls. Walk through an indiscriminate arch and you enter a courtyard garden surrounded by arch-covered walkways leading off to beautiful, palatial rooms.

A royal master suite with a contemporary Moroccan feel.

1

2

3

Paint the room in butternut (1), and add wooden shutters at the windows in chameleon (3).

Upholster the bed and any seating in sandy cream (2) linen or cotton. Cover the bed in orange-cream (4) and gorgeous souk yellow (5) cotton throws, and use the same colors for luxurious silk cushions.

4

5

Complete this contemporary look with dark-wood and rattan furniture and a selection of authentic accessories in orange-cream and chameleon.

Wilderness

Lost in a deep, dark forest, with mile upon mile of dense woodland and undergrowth—brown is the color of the wilderness. Naturally found as the color of leather, wood and earth, it is a stable tone that works in an abundance of situations. It is a practical and useful color for the home and sits well with hints of blue and green, as well as spicier reds and yellows.

Primitive *lines*

Brown is a common tone in contemporary neutral schemes.

Brown is a great, rich staple color, reminiscent of wood and leather. The color of the earth and abundant in nature, brown is less harsh than black and works fabulously as the darker component of a modern scheme, bringing warmth to any room.

The base color for this palette, exquisitely rich bitter chocolate (1), is incredibly versatile. It works incredibly well with contrasting bright accents for a modern look, or with understated neutrals for timeless elegance.

In an entrance hall, use the bitter chocolate for a few key items of furniture, such as a console table and old leather chair. Paint the walls in light rain (2) to freshen up the space, with army green (3) and taupe (5) curtains or shades.

Position a pair of lamps or vases in pink clay (4) and taupe to lift the dark furniture.

Scorched *earth*

Browns are warm and earthly, pinks lively and feminine. Pink loves brown and brown loves pink, so mix the natural qualities and earth tones of browns with warm pinks, and combine with luxurious fabrics and textures for a beautiful, romantic bedroom.

Browns and pinks are perfectly balanced in a romantic bedroom.

Base your design around a fabulous wallpaper or fabric in tones of silver-pink (2) and bitter chocolate (1). Paper the bedside wall or hang panels of fabric behind the bed for a more sumptuous feel.

Choose select pieces of furniture in bitter chocolate to set off the pink, and a plain fabric in silver-pink for window shades.

Paint the remaining walls in pale, dreamlike cloud (3), and introduce tones of fiery ginger (4) and warm red spice (5) in accessories, such as lamps, ceramics and other textiles.

African *safari*

Layer tones, patterns, and natural textures for a modern lounge.

There is a certain theme or style associated with the word "safari": khaki-colored clothing, pith helmets and animal skin. While this scheme steers clear of animal prints, it does take reference from these colors and the natural tones of the African wilderness.

A versatile set of colors that can be used in a range of different ways; contrast the lighter colors of white (2) and calico (4) with the harsher brown tones of deep chestnut (1) and barely black (3). Use a single color, perhaps tarragon (5), as a bold accent to these true neutrals.

Layer the look on a sofa, picking the main upholstery fabric in deep chestnut linen and adding textured cushions in barely black cotton, calico silk, and white felt. Add a simple tarragon throw on the arm.

Animal *tones*

The land of sunlight, wildlife, and scenic grandeur, Africa conjures up powerful images. Imagine the heat, a seemingly endless landscape, a leopard pursuing a wildebeest, or a pack of lions feasting on their catch. Take inspiration from the colors and design of animal skins, but take care not to overdo it.

Use the elements of animal print for a wild design.

Cover one wall, or area of wall, in a textured paper, or paper-backed fabric, that echoes an animal print in rich deep chestnut (1).

Set off this fabulous feature with bright gray (4) contemporary simple furniture. Add a flash of vibrant deep amber (2) in the form of a single large cushion, abstract picture or chair.

Finish the design with soft fabrics in simple plains or weaves using the subtle tones of peach-orange (3) and maroon (5).

Nature *untouched*

For inspired color choices, simply look out of the window.

A single leaf in fall may be all the inspiration you need. Take note of how yellows, browns and greens mingle together in the garden to form a beautiful and perfectly balanced scene, and echo these tones for a sunny open-plan kitchen.

1

2

3

Use tiles in energizing green stone (4), and paint the remaining wall space in gold tint (2). Accentuate the green tones with crisp, fresh striped cotton curtains in olive (5) and gold tint.

4

Choose burnt umber (1) as the color for a chunky kitchen table and kitchen units. This may darken and close the room slightly, but you can lighten and bring sunshine into the room by including countertops and matching chairs in rising sun (3).

5

To finish, include cookware and bright, pretty dinnerware in any of the accent colors.

Natural *texture*

Dark browns aren't the obvious choice for bathrooms, but bathroom furniture in burnt umber can look sophisticated and sleek against pale neutrals such as almond white and voile. A thoughtfully designed bathroom in these colors will look stunning.

The perfect scheme for a classic, regal bathroom.

Choose a beautiful traditional wood vanity unit in burnt umber (1) with a chunky natural stone top in voile (3). Keep tiles neutral in a similar tone to the voile.

Paint the remaining wall space in almond white (2), and for the window dressing, pick out a striped fabric in apricot cream (5) with a narrow Amazon blue (4) stripe running through it.

Include an assortment of fluffy towels in almond white and apricot cream, and finish with a woven wicker laundry basket in either almond white or burnt umber.

Deserted *beach*

*Take inspiration
from a beach walk.*

Walking for hours along a deserted beach is an exhilarating experience, allowing you time to contemplate. You can make meaningful keepsakes of a trip to the beach: photograph your children's foot- and handprints in the sand, and hang them up the stairs or in a hallway.

Employ this natural, energizing scheme within your home and capture the invigoration of the great outdoors.

Paint the walls in clay (1) and pick out a feature wall in garden green (4), using this hue as the backdrop to your photo gallery. Frame the images from your beach trip in tones of white clay (2) and dark mud (3) and hang.

Use khaki brown (5) for flooring that will complement the greens and neutrals. In an entrance hall you may want to include some tall floor vases in white clay.

Earth *water*

The decoration of a home office should be as carefully considered as any other room in the home to ensure it is a pleasant place to work. This scheme centers around bold accents of blue—a color associated with calm and clear thinking, and thus ideal for a working environment.

Brown tones accented with perky blues to cheer up a workspace.

1

2

3

Starting with a base color of clay (1) for the walls, choose homely storage such as painted wood furniture in fresh spring water (3) shelved with boxes and files in deeper tones, such as peppermint (2) and bitter chocolate (5). The warm tones of the browns will sit wonderfully well with these cool accents of varying intensities.

4

5

Instead of choosing a conventional desk, find a small table in natural (4) wood and use a comfortable upholstered chair in beautiful, fresh peppermint.

Hermit's *cove*

Sensual, comforting and warming shades evoke relaxation.

At times we all need an escape—a chance to get back to nature and a simpler way of life. Take inspiration from the life of a hermit; implement this warm, cozy group of colors in a snug or quiet corner of your home, and enjoy some relaxing time alone.

1

2

3

Pick out a wallpaper with a floral design in gorgeous silver birch (1) and wild rose (4) for at least one wall, and paint the remaining walls in silver birch.

Choose a velvety sofa or daybed in neutral taupe (3) cushioned with rich ivory (2) and muted dogwood (5). Layer textures wherever possible; this will further the sumptuous, cozy feel of the room.

4

5

Turn off the main lights and use lamps with dogwood shades that diffuse the light.

Wood *love*

One of nature's great fruits, the varying textures and colors of wood mean it has always featured prominently in home decoration. If you love the natural feel and tones of wood use them. Mix antique with new, blond with dark and smooth with rough.

Complementary or contrasting, wood tones work well together.

1

2

3

In a dining room, make the focal point a wooden table in teak (5) stain, and dress the center with wooden vases or accessories in mud (2) tones. Complement this with a dark-wood sideboard.

Upholster chairs in pale olive (3) with mud stained legs. Keep things simple: let the wood do the talking and paint the walls in neutral silver birch (1).

4

5

Add simple accessories, such as a pair of ceramic lamps in white clay (4), which will look great against the wood and silver birch backdrop.

Breaking *ice*

A mix of warm and cool for a masculine bedroom.

The word "ice" is somewhat contradictory in a section that centers around the warm tones of the wilderness, but this scheme is about contrast. Surround khaki with the complementary but cooler tones of lilacs and blues in a luxurious bedroom that is sensual but innately masculine.

1

2

3

Pick out a beautiful, subtle wallpaper, perhaps with metallic hints, in shades of white-lilac (2) and khaki (1). Against this, place rich dark furniture in mud (3), for example, in the form of a stunning contemporary four-poster bed.

4

Hang generous lengths of fabulous flowing silk in regal blue (4) and steel blue (5) at the windows.

5

Upholster a chaise longue in the corner of the room in a silk or velvet khaki fabric, with a beautiful patterned cushion in tones of steel blue and white-lilac.

Snow *crystals*

Browns are wonderful shades for cozy living rooms—they bring warmth into any room—although they can also darken and close a space. Use the contrasting crisp white accents of this palette to balance the scheme and inject a light, fresh feel.

Warm up snowy whites and wintry grays with warm brown tones.

Khaki (1) is a perfectly behaved deep neutral that works well for walls, furniture and upholstery. In a grown-up lounge, use it as a main paint color with panels of white (3) silk adorning a single wall. This will reflect light and brighten the room.

In front of the white paneling place a warm stone (5) sofa in a vintage leather or suede material.

Accent the room with white furniture and accessories in soft lavender (4) and iced gray (2). Glass tables and lamp bases would also complement nicely.

New *dawn*

*Furnishings need
not be restricted
to interiors.*

Opening the curtains to reveal a glorious new dawn is a joy. As sunlight spills into the room, we are drawn to the outside. This beautiful selection of colors invites you to take the beauty of the inside outside. Modern weather-resistant fabrics and furniture allow you to extend your color palette and design ideas to your yard or balcony.

1

2

3

4

5

Choose hard-wearing rattan or wicker furniture in ginger root (1), and soften it up with masses of different cushions, some of them large enough to double as floor cushions and in a vibrant color such as pink glow (2). Put a pergola in brown stone (5) over the seating area, with a gorgeous canopy in natural light (4).

Place muted mahogany (3) glass storm lanterns all around, and light with candles when the evenings creep in and the sun disappears.

Hot *sands*

Moving to the warmer orange-based browns and reminiscent of an exotic, hot, arid landscape, this scheme centers around yet more natural, earthly tones. The palette emits warmth, but the boldness of ginger root and nectar could be used in a fun and exciting way to suit a family-friendly living space.

Spice up a neutral base with warm oranges and yellows.

1

2

3

Use ginger root (1) as a practical paint color, with large sofas in a hard-wearing nectar (5) fabric. Fill the center of the room with a fun rug in tones of honeysuckle (2), beige (3), nectar and ginger root, and pick chunky tables and sideboards in dark wood (4), with plenty of cupboards and drawers.

4

5

Be creative with lighting and hang three large pendants at differing heights in the center of the room, one in honeysuckle; one in dark wood and the last in nectar, so the space feels designed but also fun and approachable.

White *smoke*

Mix smoky grays and brighter accents for a modern kitchen.

A paler version of khaki, bamboo is another very good neutral that can transcend numerous color schemes and applications. In this scheme the hue is teamed with a real mix of accents (both warm and cool) for a sleek, contemporary kitchen.

1

2

3

Paint cupboards in ash (2) and try cool silver-green (3) as a tile color. These colors will look fantastic against bamboo (1) colored walls.

Moving into the dining area of the kitchen, deepen the wall color to dark stone (4). This will intensify the space in a gentle way.

4

5

Choose ash shades for the windows with a shot of silver-green, and add ember (5) accessories sparingly.

Quiet *noise*

Neutral tones are easy to live with and can evolve into different schemes or styles easily, so it is possible to have a base neutral that runs throughout the house. By simply changing accent colors it's possible to change the whole feel of a room.

Make an impact without being garish.

1

2

3

In an open-plan space, keep the basic upholstery in bamboo (1) and furniture in warm black (5).

Make simple Roman blinds for the windows in natural (2) fabric, and add a honey (3) and warm black rug to centralize the seating space and make it a real feature of the room.

4

Add a large floor vase in kidney bean (4), and on the other side of the room, place a smaller kidney bean lamp on a table to mirror the larger one.

5

Handmade *fabric*

Neutrals and natural materials walk hand in hand.

Natural materials are not perfect and will invariably have flaws and imperfections. But if you love their true textures and how they look and behave, then use them in your interiors regardless, as these imperfections can add to their charm and will lead to a unique finished look.

1

2

3

4

5

In a lounge or living area, use hemp (1) as the base for your wall color, and hang simple true calico (2) curtains from beautiful wooden poles in gray-green (5) at the window.

Pick out a natural seagrass or wood floor in a hemp shade, and use moody eggplant (4) as a natural dyed fabric for sofas and seating.

For added texture and a touch of luxury in the scheme, add cushions in silk (3) and gray-green velvet.

Frayed *edge*

When designing a room you may feel the need to be symmetrical, neat and ordered. Employing a scheme will no doubt have you striving for perfection, but just remember that not everything has to be perfect. Distressed finishes can look smart and work well in a bedroom or lounge.

Discard perfection for a unique, lived-in look.

1

2

3

Use hemp (1) as a wall color, providing a neutral base for distressed furniture. Paint the furniture in warm stone (2) and give it a distressed finish. Use another neutral, dark stone (3), as a floor covering, whether carpet, wood or seagrass.

4

5

Nudging toward pink, cover an old chair in a distressed dusky pink (4) fabric, and hang curtains in brown-pink (5) on distressed warm stone curtain poles.

Keep lighting low and diffused with floor and table lamps, rather than a main central fitting.

Starry *night*

Incorporate elements of the night sky in a contemporary kitchen.

When the clouds clear, the midnight blue sky is a natural wonder that twinkles with bright metallic stars. Perhaps it's the unknown that makes it so magical and alluring. Take inspiration from the night sky with this thoroughly modern kitchen.

1

2

3

Choose ecru (1) as a base color for kitchen units, and use night sky (4) as a contrasting tone for all countertops. Paint walls in a mix of soft bark (2) and white (3), pinpointing where you want your eye to be led with the soft bark.

4

Keep flooring natural in lighter shades of either ecru or soft bark.

5

To complete the scheme, accessorize with light fixtures, handles and other finishing touches in burnished nickel (5) for a sleek, modern feel.

Breaking *daylight*

Hazy tones are what make neutrals work, crossing the line from a true color into an ambiguous description. Is it gray, green or beige? Ecru is a deliciously soft and amiable neutral, edging toward brown with a hint of pink, making it a versatile shade. Team with light accents to recreate the feel of the morning haze.

A fresh, sunny look for a modern lounge.

1

2

3

In a lounge, carpet the floor in ecru (1) with flecks of olive (4), and paint or paper the walls in ecru also.

Choose olive for main pieces of upholstered furniture and accent them with highlights of yellow sand (5) and green haze (3).

4

Hang a large central pendant with an olive shade in the center of the room, and mix painted furniture in buff (2) with wooden pieces in oak.

5

Any of these accent shades will be perfect for soft furnishings and accessories, so experiment.

Ice cream

The prettiest of all tones, pink is typically used in
feminine interior spaces. To avoid getting too sickly
sweet, mix these shades with moody grays and stony
neutrals. Soft, warm and comforting, the gentle, relaxed
tones of these milky ice-cream colors are perfect for
living spaces and for promoting sweet dreams.

Black *cherry*

Rich cherry accented with cool shades for an elegant bedroom.

Inspired by the deep color of a bulging bunch of black cherries, this scheme combines a real mix of hues. The cool tones of pink-gray perfectly complement indulgent, intense black cherry, and make for a flawless scheme .

For an expressive black cherry (1) bedroom let slinky silk and vibrant velvets collide, while keeping the walls and flooring neutral in stone white (4).

Make an oversized buttoned headboard in black cherry velvet, and layer the bed with sumptuous silks and satins in varying tones of pink-gray (2, 3).

Hang lengths of black cherry silk at the windows, and keep furniture to a minimum in expensive-looking dark oak (5).

Blackcurrant *sorbet*

Choosing to be adventurous with color in a kitchen can really pay off. The kitchen is the room that families probably spend the most time in, and it is increasingly becoming the main living area. Employing these colors in a carefully designed scheme will give you a kitchen to be proud of.

Strong colors in a spacious kitchen make a real statement.

For a real difference, use black cherry (1) for bold kitchen units with a contrasting bespoke toughened-glass countertop and backsplash in orchid (2).

Keep the walls neutral with a warming shade of light stone (3). A floor covering in this same shade, or one with a similar intensity, will prevent the room from becoming too dark or closed in. Accent with hints of deep blackcurrant (4) and green stone (5) in any soft furnishings and accessories.

Summer *berries*

Inject warmth into a room with these berry-inspired colors.

The components of this palette are bold, bright and daring. There is no doubt that they will warm a cold or large room, but play with balance when using shades that are all quite robust, making sure you don't use the colors in equal measure, otherwise the effect could feel heavy and over the top.

1

2

3

In a chilly lounge or drawing room, paper or paint the walls in mulberry (1) and the woodwork in soothing vanilla cream (2).

Use gorgeous vanilla bean (3) as a floor covering; in a cold room, a soft carpet would be best.

4

For main sofas or seating use khaki green (4), and for the odd occasional chair pick a different fabric in bramble fruits (5).

5

Accessorize with any of the accent shades, and add plenty of mirrors to maximize on light.

Turkish *delight*

Think of the powdery pink icing and fragrant, transparent rose of Turkish delight. To conjure up a concoction of these delicious flavors at home, surround mulberry with subtle pinks in a hallway and create an inviting entrance.

Immerse yourself in the delicate flavors of rose and the mystery of Turkey.

Paint paneling in milky coffee (4) with deep mulberry (1) walls above. Carpet in luxurious, rich cocoa (5) flecked with hints of mulberry; chocolates always work well with pinks.

Add painted furniture in sugar ice (3) and large pendant lampshades in cocoa (5).

To complete the scheme, accessorize with pretty floral prints in sugar ice or milky coffee frames and real flowers in rose water (2) vases.

Fruits *of the forest*

A scheme to unite a sunroom with the rest of the house.

Sunrooms are often overlooked as a room in the home because people only use them in the summer months, while the rest of the year they remain shut off from the main house. But a little extra love and decorative consideration will make a sunroom more appealing, so you'll want to use it all year round.

1

2

3

Simple tricks to make a sunroom feel like a part of the house include running the same flooring through from the connecting room or hallway, so it appears as an extension rather than a separate room, and plastering the interior rather than leaving it as brick.

4

Paint the plastered walls in warm stone (3) and put down a wooden floor in rich pip (4).

5

Use lychee (1) as the main color focus of the room in upholstery, and accent this with chiffon (2) and cherry (5).

Exotic *flavors*

This range of gorgeous, rich tones is offset by the calm, delicate accents of the scheme. To infuse the bedroom with elements of the exotic, paint or paper the walls in lychee and hang oriental prints and fabrics in contemporary box frames painted in pistachio.

Stylized florals and dark lacquer furniture for a lavish look.

1

2

3

For furniture, choose bitter chocolate (3) in a lacquered-wood finish with self-colored or pistachio (5) handles to further the opulent look.

Choose bedding in rich vanilla bean (2), and find a jade tone such as green marl (4) to mix with lychee (1) for a floral throw and silk cushions. Layering textures and colors will add to the plush feel.

4

5

Finish with a bitter chocolate floor vase filled with branches of pussy willow.

Delicate *balance*

A thoughtful mix of pinks for a tasteful kitchen.

It is unusual for people to use pinks in an environment such as a kitchen or dining room for fear that it will look too childish or girly. However, when used with restraint, pinks can be very elegant and really enhance a space.

In a kitchen-dining room, keep a theme running from kitchen to dining space by using coffee cream (3) for a wood countertop and wood dining table. Paint a gray-rose (1) wall in the kitchen area and mirror this in the dining space with gray-rose shades or curtains at the windows. Paint the rest of the wall space in ash (5) to keep it light and fresh.

Add coffee cream shelves in the kitchen area with pretty lilac-white (4) and plaster pink (2) ceramics displayed or stacked there, as a practical but attractive storage solution.

Elderflower *and rose*

In folklore, the elderflower was supposed to ward off evil influence. Today it is most commonly used in herbal teas or soft drinks. This scheme takes reference from its delicate flavor, combining it with rose for a refreshing, fragrant infusion of colors that's perfect for a lounge.

Treat a tired lounge with a mix of pinks and citrus.

1

2

3

Paint walls in gray-rose (1) and for a contemporary feel, use gray-rose with bright, refreshing chartreuse (5) as a striped fabric for a sofa. Carpet the area in dark stone (2) with an elderflower (3) tufted wool rug in front of the seating.

4

Cover a large footstool in zingy lemon cream (4) and use in place of a coffee table. Add curved glass side tables at either end of the sofa, and let a large abstract painting bring all the colors together on the wall.

5

Noisette *twist*

A peachy neutral looks great next to a mix of browns.

The warm tones of brown look fantastic with both oranges and pinks. Butternut pink, is a delightful combination of both colors and will work wonderfully when mixed with a range of brown tones.

1

2

3

To create a contemporary twist in a traditional bathroom, paint the outside of a fabulous claw-foot tub in butternut pink (1) and finish with grayed ivory (2) feet.

4

5

Set the bath off against a distressed wood floor in brown olive (5), and paint walls in grayed ivory. If you need to tile a shower area or backsplash, choose a glazed pale walnut-colored (4) tile.

Mix accessories and towels in tones of butternut pink, chestnut (3) and pale walnut, and mount a traditional framed gilt mirror on the wall to reflect light and add a touch of class.

Old *creamery*

Butternut pink is a welcoming and interesting color choice
for a dining room, and, mixed with neutrals such as grayed
ivory and light stone, it can create an elegant but relaxed
space. Keep decoration simple, with the main focus
on the dining table.

*In a classic dining
room, keep the
setting simple.*

1

2

3

Paint the walls of the room
butternut pink (1) for an inviting
backdrop. Choose feature lighting
to highlight the warmth of
butternut pink; clotted
cream (4) wall lights with dark
morello (5) silk shades
will work fantastically
well. Include a matching
morello pendant shade
for over a wooden
morello dining table.

4

5

Accentuate the wall
color further by
installing a light stone
(3) fireplace mantel with grayed
ivory (2) candelabras on each
corner. Keep floor covering
light, in either grayed ivory or
light stone.

English *toffee*

Colors to give an open-plan apartment a homely atmosphere.

In today's modern world, a large part of interior design centers around contemporary style: sleek, sophisticated decor and open-plan spaces. While modern and stylish, it can sometimes be difficult to make large open-plan apartments feel homely. Let this scheme show you how.

Candy (1) is a light-reflecting color that will give a warm glow to any space. Mix candy on the walls, and include furniture and seating in flat gray (3) and pebbled cream (4).

Carpet or cover the floor in a practical material and color such as flat cocoa (5), because in an open-plan space it will need to put up with a high level of traffic.

To finish, add a bright injection of color with momentary flashes of deep pink (2), for example, in the form of a modern lamp in the corner of the lounge.

Crème *caramel*

Sometimes rooms have to be adaptable for multiple uses.
For example, an office cum guest bedroom needs to be efficient
and practical but welcoming and attractive at the same time.
Using neutrals with warm tones and delicate pinks will help
to take the focus away from
working environments.

A clever scheme to combine both work and rest.

1

2

3

Carpet the room in candy (1) and
paint the walls in clotted cream
(5). Pick a compact sofa bed in
neutral caramel (4) and dress with
mauve gray (2) and beautiful
butternut pink (3) cushions.

Be clever with furniture
and choose a pretty
table rather than a
conventional desk
and a cupboard that can
double as a wardrobe.

4

Add shelves painted
in candy, and use rattan
storage boxes to hide stationery
and other work accoutrements.

5

Strawberry *mousse*

Strawberry cream will gel with most schemes and won't tire or date.

People frequently decorate rooms to update a look. A scheme or look at the height of fashion won't remain there forever. Selecting a scheme that won't date is a challenge, but using a neutral base is normally a good start.

1

2

3

4

5

Moving more into browny pinks, strawberry cream (1) is a great base neutral for just about any interior space.

In a lounge, paint walls in strawberry cream, and keep it fresh and light with natural gray (2) floors and linen (3) shades or shutters at the windows.

Edge a strawberry cream linen chair with a hazlenut (4) trim for upholstery that's contemporary and fresh. Choose a low-level modern sofa in light teal (5), and add large strawberry cream linen square cushions and smaller hazlenut velvet bolster cushions.

Coffee *bean*

Imagine the delicious aroma of roasted coffee beans. This scheme takes inspiration from the deep, rich brown color of the beans themselves and the harmonious color of the red coffee cherries from which they derive. Employ these colors in a family living area.

Use these dark accent shades in a family lounge or children's playroom.

Paint the walls of your chosen room in strawberry cream (1).

For furniture, pick chunky leather sofas in coffee bean (3) to sit on a funky blood orange (5) carpet. Adorn with scatter cushions in shades of cappuccino (2) and pot pink (4). Use these accent shades in a large geometric pattern for shades or curtains also.

Add fun beanbags in cappuccino for the children to lounge on and as a practical solution for unexpected visitors.

Thai *magic*

Subtle pink tones punctuated by exotic, vibrant accents.

For a grown-up but decadently girly bedroom for a teenager, use these understated pinks with dark wood furniture. The voluptuousness of pink works perfectly with the richness of the browns, creating an incredibly warming and welcoming room.

1

2

3

Paint the walls of the room in delicate orchid (1), with a feature wall of paper in beautiful opal (2) and cotton candy (5).

Choose a grown-up warm brown (3) bed frame and simple wood furniture in the same finish. Use opal for bed linen and any of the accent colors for cushions.

4

5

Break up the pink by hanging a show-stoppingly large Thai green (4) shade in the center of the room, and accessorize with strings of lights, Buddha statues and potted orchids.

Eastern *rose*

In this unusual group of colors, the gentle pink tinge of delicate orchid is played down by the use of browny neutrals and blue-toned flint, in a contemporary scheme that would suit an open-plan kitchen area.

A modern scheme that you may not naturally put together.

1

2

3

Paint the walls in delicate orchid (1) and use vanilla (4) and warm cream (3) for kitchen cabinets.

Choose dark stone (5) as a tile or wood tone for flooring to contrast nicely against the light kitchen units. Dark stone would also work as a color for countertops.

4

5

Pick out warm cream for simple shades with dark stone wooden pulls on the bottom, and accessorize with flint (2) ceramics and cookware for a subtle hint of gray-blue.

Pink *pistachio*

Soft, creamy tones to promote relaxation.

Emulate the smooth, velvety touch of a petal with pretty pinks and creamy pistachios. This gentle combination will work well in relaxed lounges, but it's also a winner in the bedroom.

1

2

3

4

5

Try the combination of peach tint (1) walls and pale pistachio (2) underfoot; the strength of color is especially similar in these shades, so they will look seamlessly beautiful together.

To dress windows, add some rich asparagus (3) and plaster (4) curtains or shades in a delicate floral or stripe.

Mirror the pale pistachio in painted furniture, and add hints of pastel orange (5) and plaster in ceramic vases and accessories.

Flower *water*

Pink is a combination of red and white, but there are so many variants. Pinks can be tinged brown, orange, yellow and gray. Peach tint has a gray edge to it, which makes it a refined and sophisticated pink tone.

Neutrals and hints of pink, perfect for a study or small lounge.

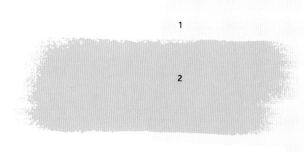

1

2

3

Play it safe and choose natural stone (2) for flooring and paint the walls in peach tint (1). This will keep the room light and airy.

With the walls and floors in these creamy shades, use the bold but elegant tone of mulberry (4) for upholstery with warm cream (3) and pink (5) polka dot cushions.

4

5

Pick out the tone of natural stone as a background color for a shade with a beautiful, fun pinky pattern.

Vanilla *story*

A pale scheme that will need loving attention to keep it pure.

Vanilla is smooth, tasty and rich. Derived from the orchid, vanilla is also a pungent scent that has been used for centuries in perfumes. It mixes well with most colors and is therefore a highly adaptable hue for decor.

1

2

3

Accentuate the orangey undertones of white-peach (1) with vanilla (4) and white lemon (2) striped cotton sofas.

At the windows hang long drapes that pool on the floor in vanilla silk.

4

Cover the center of the room with a luscious brown velvet (5) shaggy rug that should feel fabulous under bare feet. Cushion the sofas in mauve hint (3) and white-peach for an understated nod to color.

5

Peach *melba*

Picture a juicy peach half surrounded in vanilla ice cream and sprinkled with hazelnut shavings. This palette is almost as soft as the last, and so good you can almost taste it. Use this scrumptious peach and pinky scheme as inspiration for a little girl's bedroom.

A delicious set of colors inspired by the classic dessert.

1

2

3

Start with a pretty wallpaper in white-peach (1) and strawberry milk (5). Above a painted orchid (3) daybed drape a cream of peach (2) voile canopy edged with pink beads, stones and crystals.

Add a collection of polka dot, floral and striped pastel cushions in mauve dust (4), strawberry milk, cream of peach and orchid.

To finish, adorn walls with painted hearts, beaded curtains and strings of lights.

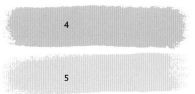

4

5

Northern lights

The matriarch of all the neutrals, cream works on so many levels. It is light, bright and clean while remaining warm and welcoming. Most Scandinavian interiors are simple and delicate with their color balance but are still inviting spaces. Use this chapter to take inspiration from Scandinavian design and landscape.

Swedish *modern*

This look works particularly well in an open-plan space.

Infamous for Modernist furniture crafted from natural materials, chiefly wood, Swedish design is beautiful, organic and highly functional. Take inspiration from this style and combine with a fairly simple color palette for a stunning overall effect.

1

2

3

4

5

Paint the walls in blond wood (1) and make simple shades or curtains in white (2) and country white (3) striped cotton. Pick plain modern sofas in black (5) leather.

Set off this basic color palette with some beautiful Swedish modernist antiques in teak (4), or find good contemporary interpretations.

Take care not to over-accessorize. Stick to a set of lamps and a beautifully designed glass or ceramic item.

Atmospheric *light*

The Scandinavian style features bleached woods, whitewashed furniture and gingham and floral textiles with a homemade feel. It can look a little cutesy if overdone, but if used thoughtfully with these selected colors they will work fantastically well in a dining room.

Take elements of rustic, homely Scandinavian design into your home.

1

2

3

Paint the walls in blond wood (1) and pick out a delicate fabric for window dressings in gorgeous Nordic cream (4).

Paint wooden chairs and a table in a wash of magnolia (5), and add tied-on seat pads in white-gray (2).

4

If you are blessed with an open fireplace, keep the mantel simple and painted magnolia with logs stacked neatly by the side.

5

Decorate the room with ceramics in deep sky (3) and white-gray, and lots of tall church candles.

Beachy *point*

Scandinavian colors are perfect for a beach house or country cottage.

The Scandinavian love of bleached woods and all things natural transcends beautifully to a seaside retreat.

Since most beach houses operate an open-plan living space, in the main sitting room paint the walls in sand (1) and elsewhere in Swedish linen (2) to make the space cozy and relaxing.

1

2

3

Choose reclaimed and Swedish or Shaker furniture in wood (4) or painted in white clay (5).

To soften a wood floor, throw down plenty of rugs in various textures and tones of neutrals with hints of a color such as lilac-white (3). These should look great and feel fabulous under bare feet.

4

5

To complete the look add candles in storm lanterns with sand in the bottom and plenty of soft cashmere throws to keep guests warm once the sun goes down.

Gustavian *styling*

Swedish Gustavian furniture is elegant yet simple. Its look is classic and can transcend both traditional and modern interiors. This group of colors attempts to do the same. Create a dreamy bedroom with an elegant Gustavian chaise longue painted and upholstered in Swedish linen.

A scheme of simple colors and design for a bedroom.

1

2

3

Take sand (1) as a natural color for a beautiful polished wood or parquet floor that will be the real star next to these muted colors.

Add a hint of glamour with an antique-looking crystal green (5) chandelier hung in the center of the room.

4

For textiles, mix checks, stripes and plain natural linens and cottons in beige (3), gingham green (4) and Swedish linen (2). Layering fabrics and textures will make the room feel comfy and cozy.

5

Textural *shades*

A scheme that allows you to make the most out of textures.

When working with a basic color palette or neutrals, introducing texture will ensure the scheme does not become bland or boring. Work with a variety of finishes and materials, such as metals, woods, cottons, linens and natural stones, and experiment to your heart's content.

1

2

3

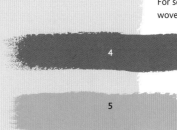

4

5

In a lounge, paint walls in suede (1) and furniture in white (3) with dull steel gray (4) handles.

For sofas, choose a textured woven Nordic cream (2) fabric and place a huge Nordic blue (5) rug in the center of the room.

Pick out key items, such as an odd vase or lampshade, in Nordic blue. Add different colored wooden frames, an upholstered footstool in steel gray suede and some crystal candlesticks for a sleek, sophisticated feel.

Nordic *charm*

Though Scandinavian interiors are generally light and based around white or neutrals, they always manage to look warm and inviting. Conjure up the image of a large open fire; imagine the crackling flames, the warmth that emanates and the cozy feeling this scene creates.

Evoke the relaxing feel of an open fire and the soft light it creates.

1

2

3

To create the same feel, use warm yellowed neutrals in a family room focused around suede (1) colored walls.

Warm beige (2) makes a practical base color for upholstery, which can be teamed with cushions in cheery lamplight (3) and muted lemon (4).

4

For a lived-in look, choose storage cupboards and side tables in antique oak (5), and accessorize with interesting but educational items, such as a huge bookcase, prints of old maps or an old globe on a stand.

5

Crystal *light*

A cool selection of colors to maximize light.

A rainbow of beautiful colors appear when light and crystal react. Take inspiration from this image and brighten up a bathroom with these light-reflecting colors and an over-the-top use of mirrors.

1

2

3

Pick a beautiful natural stone in pinky buff (1) for both floor and wall tiles. Paint any remaining wall space in neutral voile (3). This should keep the room light, airy, and fresh.

4

Choose pure, clean white (2) for furniture and sanitary ware.

5

To increase the room's light, source a collection of both new and antique mirrors in varying framed finishes painted silver-gray (4). Use ice blue (5) and silver-gray as the colors for towels and accessories.

Warm *glow*

A traditional Scandinavian folk scheme in a girl's bedroom will make it warm, welcoming and homely. Go back in time with fleece throws, wooden animals, knitted teddy bears and old-fashioned peg boards.

A fun folk scheme to excite any child.

1

2

3

Start by painting the walls of the room in pinky buff (1) and furniture in a white (4) wash.

Choose a wrought-iron black (5) bed and pile it high with cushions in pinky buff and red wash (2) gingham and pale blue (3) and white stripes. With "busy" cushions keep bed linen plain and simple, perhaps in pale blue.

4

5

Pick a pretty floral in muted pastels for a seat pad on a small wooden chair in the corner, and use the same fabric for the window dressing.

Milk *and honey*

*Try a lighter,
brighter approach
to the dining room.*

Honey is a fabulous warm neutral; its yellow undertones make it very adaptable and stop it from looking cold. Although a favorite for kitchen schemes and perhaps not the normal choice for a dining room, honey looks great with woods and whitewashed furniture.

1

2

3

Position a large trestle-style white (2) washed and distressed dining table on bleached wood (3) floorboards. This will look great against honey (1) walls.

4

5

Use pale iris white (4) to paint wooden chairs in varying shapes and sizes, and place a pair of decorative crystal candlesticks on the dining table.

For curtains, pick a light cotton voile in iris white and simple wrought-iron poles. For a flash of color, upholster the seat pads in red wash (5) cotton.

Sweet *surprise*

Picture a jar of sweet and viscous golden honey and you'll see the inspiration behind this scheme. The warm golden yellow is soothing and tranquil and will work in any number of settings but is perfect for a child's nursery because the color can easily be adapted as the child grows.

Use wholesome honey as a rich, warm base color.

1

2

3

Paint the walls in wholesome honey (1), and, in traditional Scandinavian style, keep the furniture painted pure white (5).

Use faded orange (2) to make a loose cover for a small comfortable armchair in the corner of the room, and add a gray-taupe (4) cotton cushion for extra comfort.

4

Hang a fabric shade for the central light in pale mauve (3), which will diffuse the light to a lovely warm glow. Find simple animal prints and hang on the walls in pure white frames to finish.

5

Distressed *edge*

Rough edges and natural colors for a rustic look.

When you choose natural stone for a bathroom or hallway, there are many finishes available. If you want to go streamlined and flush pick a filled and straight-edge tile, but if you want a rustic feel choose a chipped-edge product.

1

2

3

In a large hallway, choose a large tile in heritage cream (1) for the whole length of the hall.

Up the stairs, run a carpet runner in mushroom (5) and ash (2) stripes. Paint the walls in muted birch (3) and curtain simply with gorgeous billowing, floor-length curtains in Nordic cream (4).

4

In a bathroom, Nordic cream units will work wonderfully against muted birch tiled or painted walls and a mushroom colored floor.

5

Evening *warmth*

If you enjoy a touch of shabby chic, try picking out a pretty floral in neutral colors and combining it with an old leather armchair, fluffy rugs and hand-knitted cushions. These colors combined with a variety of textures will result in a room centered around comfort.

Sometimes a room looks better if it's a little lived in.

1

2

3

Paint the main walls in heritage cream (1) and re-cover an old armchair or sofa in a distressed, hot chocolate (4) leather.

Pick a floral fabric in tinted cream (2) and bleached sun (5) natural linen, and use this to cover cushions.

4

Paint the woodwork and fireplace mantel in natural linen (3), and place picture frames and plants around the room. Use a variety of shapes, sizes and finishes for the accessories, so that they look like they've been collected over time.

5

Looking *for light*

Ideas and colors to make a basement feel more spacious.

If you need to brighten up a basement lounge or workroom, use mirrors to capture and throw light around. Not only do they reflect light, but they also increase the feeling of space. If ceiling height is an issue, which is often the case in basements, use pot lights or wall lights.

1

2

3

Paint all the walls in ivory (1) and follow similarly with white (2) for all the woodwork. At the windows choose uniform shades or shutters in muslin (4).

For the main upholstery play between ice (3) and ash (5), keeping scale in mind so as not to overpower the space.

4

5

Finally, hang mirrors where they reflect interesting vistas and can bounce around the light from the windows, and bring some low-maintenance plants inside—they'll make the space seem more organic and lived in.

Peaceful *dusk*

To enjoy the view as the last light of day streams through the window, make a quiet spot you can relax in. Position a wrought-iron (4) daybed filled with cushions of all shapes and sizes in the place where you have the best view—perhaps this is a landing or an area in a bedroom.

A range of soft, subtle tints for a restful space.

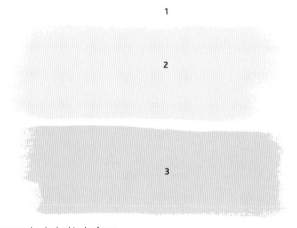

1

2

3

To ensure the daybed is the focus of the space, keep the surrounding walls neutral in ivory (1), and use dark stone (3) as the color for floor covering.

Make cushions from soft pink (5) woven linen with mother-of-pearl buttons, dark stone suede, with spots in lilac moon (2), and ivory silk with crystal studs. Use these to add texture to the daybed.

4

5

Position a bookshelf or magazine rack nearby so the area feels like it has a purpose.

Scandinavian *style*

A subtle, Nordic color palette, perfect for a formal lounge.

Nordic colors are gentle and inoffensive, so they make a great basis for a traditional setting with period detailing, such as a grand marble fireplace and elegant cornice. A muted palette such as this is extremely versatile and will enable you to inject your own styling.

1

2

3

4

5

Paint the walls in warm, glorious Nordic cream (1), before washing a wood floor in white (5).

Furnish the room with stonewash (2) upholstery and antique furniture in dark oak (4). Include a range of found objects, such as wooden statues, vases and masks.

Accessorize and add texture to the scheme with soft furnishings in Nordic cream and lime white (3) cottons and silks.

Natural *lines*

This simple yet serious scheme would work especially well in a modern renovation or open-plan apartment. Use the softness of Nordic cream and the weightier accents of this palette and take the austere modernist style into a contemporary kitchen.

Serious, sophisticated color choices for a modern kitchen.

1

2

3

Use Nordic cream (1) as your base color and pick out shiny chrome (4) appliances and hardware.

Choose chrome-legged stools or chairs with black (2) leather seats and contrast light ivory (3) kitchen units with black granite for the countertops.

For a sleek injection of color choose olive (5) for neat roller or Roman shades and as a base color for abstract artworks on the walls.

4

5

White heat

Imagine snowflakes falling through the last light of the day, colors changing through pale yellow and barely-there pinks and warming the freezing air. White is sexy yet clean and virginal. Drawing on all of the color sections, pick out the lightest "white" shades in each palette and contrast and complement the purest of all the neutrals. It is amazing how the tiniest hint of color can change and impact the ambience of a space.

Gentle *whites*

For a calming and personable interior choose fresh neutrals.

Fresh, light and crisp neutrals create a summery scheme that works well all year round. Gray ice is a thoroughly modern shade and makes a great base for these citrus tints of lemon and lime. This pale, contemporary palette choice will help you create an airy, spacious feel in any room.

1

2

3

Introduce the scheme into an open-plan kitchen-dining room, with gray ice (1) walls and lime white (2) painted kitchen units.

Simple, clean gray-white (3) countertops in a natural marble will work well with this scheme, and you can bring focus to the dining or sitting area area by painting a wall in pale lemon (4).

4

5

For non-painted furniture, choose a natural oak (5) finish and a simple shaker style to ensure the scheme stays light and bright.

Masculine *detail*

A plain backdrop will increase the feeling of space within a small property. When space is important you have to be careful with furniture, so be practical and don't try to squeeze in too many pieces or items that are too big. Ideal for a studio apartment or an inner-city crash pad, introducing navy gives a masculine edge to this palette.

Combine neutrals with dark accents for an ultra-sleek scheme.

Paint the walls in gray ice (1) and carpet throughout in warm, neutral biscuit (3).

For a touch of sleek sophistication choose navy (2) for sofa upholstery and scatter some simple cotton cushions in biscuit and pure white (4).

Finish with black and white prints in large charcoal (5) frames for sharp and stylish yet uncomplicated decoration.

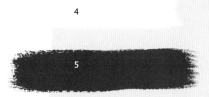

Tonal *change*

A perfect partnership of pinks and grays.

Pinks are warm and inviting, but toned in this way and teamed with grays they can also look modern and chic. To give a contemporary twist to the traditional "girly pink" bedroom, choose a harmonious combination of warm gray-whites and dusky pinks.

1

2

3

Paint the bedhead wall in dark blush (5) and the remaining walls in winter white (1). Paint wooden floorboards in either winter white or light blush (3).

Upholster the headboard in light blush silk and use the same fabric to make dress cushions.

4

5

Choose good-quality cotton bed linen in orchid white (2) and add texture and a touch of luxury with a sateen bed throw in medium blush (4). Accessorize with glass perfume bottles and silver candlesticks.

Natural *stone*

A bathroom should appear clean, fresh and light. If the room is not blessed with a flood of natural sunlight, then you need to implement a scheme that capitalizes on that which is available. Natural stone and neutral whites are simple but effective when creating a light and airy contemporary bathroom.

Keep colors and materials basic for a sophisticated bathroom.

1

2

3

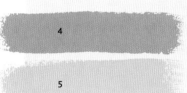

Use winter white (1) marble wall tiles and paint any remaining wall space in pure white (2).

To bring warmth to the room, lay a wood floor in oak (4) and choose free-standing sink units, also in oak.

Make the most of the bright white space by placing a large mirror framed in oak on the largest wall. Mirrors are a great way to maximize a room's light source.

Accessorize with a range of towels in peached ivory (3), pure white and pale sage (5).

Bright *splash*

Jazz up a neutral kitchen with flashes of vibrant color.

A great way to make a neutral scheme fun and family-friendly is to add bright, bold injections of color. If you like to change the feel of a space through the seasons this is an ideal scheme for you, because cushions and accessories can be mixed and matched accordingly.

1

2

3

4

5

In a family kitchen or dining area paint the walls in a hard-wearing blush (1) and choose kitchen units in pure white (2), which look particularly great in a high-gloss finish. For flooring opt for hard-wearing seagrass or natural stone (3) tiles.

Now for the fun part. Cushion alternate chairs in fuchsia (4) and pea green (5), and add brightly colored ceramic vases and dishes in the same bright shades. Finally, frame your favorite children's pictures in an informal gallery on the gorgeous blush walls.

Calm *neutrals*

Choose natural fabrics such as wool, cotton, linen and silk for an array of furniture and soft furnishings. If you have a fireplace, make it the focal point of the room by positioning seating around the hearth, making it inviting and comfortable.

For a warm and cozy neutral lounge add texture and interest.

1

2

3

Pick a white butter (2) finish for the fireplace, either painted or stone, and paint or paper the walls in blush (1).

Carpet the room in a textured light taupe (3), something that looks and feels great, and use mouse (4) and gray clay (5) as shades for sofas and chairs.

4

5

Dress windows in billowing curtains in either white butter or mouse, and find beautiful mohair throws in blush to rest on the arms of sofas for chilly winter evenings.

Cluster *of pink*

A scheme centered around contrast.

This palette is based around the juxtaposition of light and dark, combining delicate accent tones with startling darks. Mixing extreme tones in this way has dramatic effects—perfect for a striking and contemporary living room.

1

2

3

For a pretty Japanese cherry-blossom-inspired room, make the star a pair of buttermilk (3) sofas. Choose velvet or silk for a glamorous edge, or stick to woven cotton for a "daytime" look.

4

As a neutralized platform for the creamy furniture, choose a warm gray (4) carpet and color walls in subtle rose-white (1).

5

Complete the look with Oriental-style dark wood or lacquered furniture in barely black (5) and accessories in white (2) and barely black.

Modernity *personified*

As the resurgence of wallpaper continues, the focus of this scheme is the wallpaper itself. Think of wallpaper as a large picture; if you can find a design you adore you'll probably never tire of it. If you have the budget or happen to be particularly artistic, you could design or commission a hand-painted wallpaper.

A clever combination of both modern and retro styles.

Find a striking wallpaper in rose-white (1) and gray clay (5) and use it on a feature wall in a lounge or dining room. Keep the remaining walls plain by painting in white clay (4), and choose a light, neutral floor covering so as not to overdo it.

For a touch of glamour, opt for modern or retro furniture and light fittings in barely black (2) with chrome (3) detailing. In a lounge, a sofa upholstered in fabulous gray clay fabric with rose-white cushions will look fabulous.

Spring *white*

Choose springtime colors for a welcoming guest bedroom.

Quiet colors allow clarity of mind and will provide guests with a relaxing place to sleep. Don't overcrowd a guest bedroom, but think practically about what your visitors will need besides a bed: a dressing table or perhaps a chest of drawers, include a few hooks for hanging clothes and a good mirror.

1

2

3

4

5

Keep flooring bright with natural cotton (1), and mirror this color in the furniture. For a subtle difference, paint the walls in lemon white (2)—the bright whites will reflect light around the room and create a feeling of space.

For a contemporary twist, paint a large, ornate framed mirror in warm stone (4), which will look great against the lemon white walls.

Add a simple Roman blind in a pattern of sandy stone (3) and rose stone (5) for a flash of color, and finish with a vase of fresh roses on the dressing table.

Chocolate *truffle*

Smooth, velvety chocolate tones are neutral and inoffensive but warm and elegant at the same time. Here they are used as soft tints, subtle and understated yet instantly gratifying and welcoming. These colors would work anywhere, but because they are so incredibly inviting, they are ideal for a hallway.

A selection of soft chocolatey tones, perfect for a hallway.

1

2

3

Consider a striped paper in natural cotton (1) and chocolate milk (3) for a classic, elegant look for a hallway or grander entrance hall.

Apply deep baseboards and paint any woodwork and stairs in pure white (4). Use a gorgeous, rich deep clay (5) carpet to give depth and lead the eye (and your guests!) through the space.

4

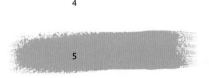

5

Accessorize with purple truffle (2) and natural cotton fabrics, and add a lantern or chandelier for a touch of glamour.

Vintage *modern*

*Take inspiration
from the past and
combine old with new.*

For a cool, serene and minimalist lounge, employ these gentle
hues and use one-off designer or vintage pieces of furniture.
Keep knicknacks to a bare minimum, and
hide clutter away in streamlined,
contemporary furniture.

1

2

3

Using a neutral backdrop of
eggshell (1) painted walls, and
add elegance and soft styling
with a beautiful chaise lounge
in bronze (3). To complement
the vintage feel of the
bronze finish, accessorize
with cushions in citrus
white (2) and iced blue
(5) in varying textures
of silks and cottons.

4

5

Keep flooring, whether
carpet or wood boards,
light and neutral in a
light shade of eggshell.

For storage solutions choose a
high-gloss, pure white (4) finish
on doors and cabinets.

Warm *whites*

White is not only the most popular paint color in the world but also the most complicated. There are simply hundreds of variations on the hue. Employ this scheme of warm whites in a space that has a double function, perhaps as a study and dining room.

Warm shades of white suit any surroundings.

1

2

3

Paper the dining area in eggshell (1) and stone white (2), while painting elsewhere in eggshell. These pale, natural colors will give a spacious feel, while the paper defines a clear change of use.

Use a hard-wearing sisal flooring in deep clay (4) as another sound neutral base. Make dramatic floor-length drapes in the dining area and a simple Roman shade in the study section in soft iris (3) and white chocolate (5), defining the different areas but retaining the overall feel of space and unity.

4

5

Unusual *combinations*

Startling accents to punctuate an almost white interior.

For a neutral, calm living space, you don't have to stick to bleached-out colors and off-whites. The best interior designs work by unusual applications and quirky surprises within a flawless scheme.

1

2

3

Paint walls in subtle ivory (1) and all woodwork and ceilings in pure white (2). At the windows, hang thick, heavy cotton drapes in vanilla taupe (3) on chunky barely black (5) curtain poles.

4

5

Use buttercup (4) to upholster an unusual chair; bright and interesting colors will make a statement, but the overall feel of the scheme is neutral and light.

Use barely black for other items of furniture.

Into *the blue*

The color of the sea and the sky, blue is a natural color, fantastic at all levels of intensity. Its cool, calming effects make it an ideal shade for a bedroom, although the lighter, fresher versions included in this scheme will work well in any type of room.

A scheme that displays the restful, calming side of blue.

1

2

3

In a traditional room that can take a chair rail without cutting the room in two, try painting below the rail in the light shade of subtle ivory (1) and above it in a blue-green tone such as barely aqua (2).

4

For flooring use warm gray (5), the darkest shade, in a smart carpet or sisal matting. For furniture or upholstery use pure white (3) to evoke a clean-lined Scandinavian feel.

5

Accessorize with barely aqua and gray-blue (4) cushions and rugs to finish.

Elegant *white*

What cleaner and more refined color is there than pure white?

While pure white can be impractical for a family environment, it has an amazing kudos within interior design. In most instances pure white is only used for ceilings and woodwork, but why not be ruthless and use it on all walls and architectural details?

1

2

3

Paint all walls, baseboards, etc., in pure white (1). Keep the majority of furniture painted pure white also.

Finding a white carpet is almost impossible, so opt for off-white (3) instead.

4

White is so incredibly neutral that it really does go with any shade. Pick out particular objects for hints of color, such as an oak chair with a sand (2) seat, a footstool in brown (5) or a warm cream (4) vase, and mix and match both colors and textures to your heart's content.

5

East *meets West*

Oriental influence in interior schemes has long graced our bedrooms and lounges. Inject your own taste of the Orient by combining a pure white base, with natural neutrals and dark woods for an elegant look that will work anywhere.

A basic yet timeless scheme inspired by the Orient.

1

2

3

In a lounge, hang pale pebble gray (3) curtains from elegant dark walnut (5) poles against pure white (1) colored walls.

Sit a pair of clotted cream (2) sofas opposite each other, and dress with symmetrical dark taupe (4) cushions.

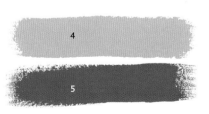

On a wood floor or plain carpet frame the sitting area with a dark taupe rug edged in clotted cream.

Accessorize with oversized dark wood lamps with shades in clotted cream, and tall, dark floor vases placed in pairs.

Muted *tones*

A palette of refined colors for an entrance hall.

In a traditional setting, mixing up muted tones for fabrics, wallpapers and upholstery works extremely well. Combine tweeds, linens, cotton prints and patterned papers in these subdued tones for a stunning overall look.

1

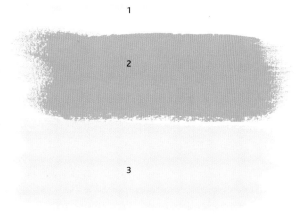

2

3

In an entrance hall, paper with a substantial patterned paper in gray-white (1) and dove gray (2). Pair the paper with a traditional woven fabric in tones of juniper (4) and gray-white.

4

5

Select an area, perhaps up the stairs, to add simple tongue-and-groove paneling and paint in calico (3).

Finally, paint an old chest or console table in pearl (5) and top with a pair of elegant lamps with calico shades. If you have the space, you may want to re-cover an old easy chair in a shabby juniper fabric.

Built-in *luxury*

The heart of a home is often reputed to be the kitchen. With an increasing amount of our time centering around this room, it is important that we implement a thoughtful scheme. If you have an open-plan area you should choose clever storage and attractive finishes for the kitchen.

A selection of both lights and darks for a sleek kitchen.

Wash the room in simple gray-white (1) as a perfect base color for the space.

Combine green oxide (2) and nickel (3) as finishes for kitchen units. Keep the nickel prominent, perhaps combining it with glass for super-sleek cupboards. Keep countertops bright, smart, clean and practical in pure white (4).

4

5

Finally, add hinted accessories in gorgeous pale aquamarine (5) for a cool, contemporary kitchen you'll want to show off.

Sun *blushed*

Fruity blushes heighten your appetite...

If you're lucky enough to have a large open-plan area, accent fruity reds, berry shades and warming whites with antiqued metallics for a luxurious atmosphere. In an open-air kitchen, even corners can be a cozy, practical living space.

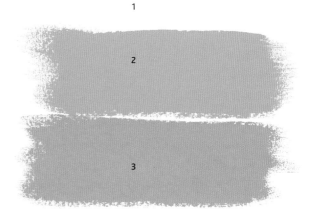

To make the most of small or awkward spaces, use purpose-built fitted seating and add storage drawers or cupboards below them. Drench the walls with serene almond white (1), and upholster the seating area in bold eggplant (5). Paint any clever storage space the same color as the walls so they blend into the background. Accessorize with cushions, vases, pictures and frames in old gold (2) and pewter (3), and use rich walnut (4) as a tone for accessories and occasional furniture, such as a nest of tables or a small bookshelf.

Index

Warming *whitewash*

In an age when more people work from home, it's important to dedicate a room or "zoned" area as a practical working space. Any location will do. But regardless of whether it's a garage, converted bedroom or simply a large crawl space under the stairs, choose colors that are easy on the eye, energizing and relaxing.

Calm colors energize your workspace.

1

2

3

4

5

A playful mix of neutrals with a balance of green is a fresh combination that will brighten as well as harmonize. Use almond white (1) as a color for all fitted and stand-alone furniture, and paint the walls in sandy cream (2). All other woodwork should be painted pure white (4). If ample natural light isn't available, add a quirky desk lamp and storage files/boxes in bright textured moss-yellow (3) for a splash of color. Finally, use orange-taupe (5) for upholstery and curtains or shades, if applicable.

How to use *this book*

1 Color-coded bullets

These color-coded bullets correspond to the color chapter that you are in.

2 Overview

Mood-enhancing words to help you imagine the feeling each scheme will evoke.

3 Inspirations

The inspiration behind the scheme's color choices.

4 Theory

The theory behind the interior-design style, and how to apply the featured scheme to a real-life interior. Find ideas and inspiration on materials and finishes, flooring, furniture, patterns and accessories.

5 Main color

The main color in the room, usually to be used on the walls, although sometimes furniture or flooring may be the main focus. Take this book into your local DIY store and ask them to match a test pot to this color. Paint a square of color onto your chosen area and let it dry, as paint always changes color when it dries. Live with the color for a day or two before committing to a whole room.

6 Accent colors

These can be used for an adjacent wall, for woodwork or to match to upholstery fabrics. The colors may be darker or lighter tones of the main shade, shades to balance a room or complementary colors that create a contrast in your chosen interior.

7 Highlight colors

These can take the form of a sharp injection of color, such as a red vase in a very neutral pale blue interior, or the final balancing tone in a range of harmonious colors, such as a rich, chocolate brown in a room of soft, creamy toffee tones. Although only used in small quantities, the highlight colors are often the most important shades of all, since they complete the design.

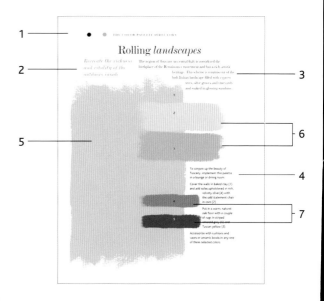

How to use *this book*

Use this handy pull-out key as a quick reference to
how each of the palettes function.

Credits

With special thanks to Heidi Best for her
contribution to the introductory part of
this book.

Quarto would like to acknowledge and thank the
following for supplying the images reproduced in
this book:

3: Lee Garland
www.leegarlandphotography.co.uk
4-5: Lee Garland
www.leegarlandphotography.co.uk
8-9: Lee Garland
www.leegarlandphotography.co.uk
10-11: Corbis
12: David George/redcover.com
13: Lee Garland
www.leegarlandphotography.co.uk
15t: Corbis
15b: Hiscox Parlade/redcover.com
16: Jean Maurice/redcover
17: Verity Welsted/redcover.com
19tl, bl: Marlborough Tiles
www.marlboroughtiles.co.uk
19tr & mr: Jane Churchill
www.janechurchill.com
19ml: Kobal collection
19bl: Larsen/www.larsenfabrics.com
19br: Shutterstock
21tl: Corbis
21tr: Jane Churchill/www.janechurchill.com
21ml: Larsen/www.larsenfabrics.com
21mr: Ketchum/www.ketchum.com
020-7611-3500
21br: Shutterstock
22: Ketchum/www.ketchum.com
020-7611-3500
23tr: Graham Atkins/redcover.com

23bl: Lee Garland
www.leegarlandphotography.co.uk
24: Ashley Morrison/redcover.com
25: Debi Treloar/redciver.com
27: Bieke Claessens/redcover.com
32: Lee Garland
www.leegarlandphotography.co.uk
52: Lee Garland
www.leegarlandphotography.co.uk
76: Lee Garland
www.leegarlandphotography.co.uk
96: Allum Callender/redcover.com
116: Lee Garland
www.leegarlandphotography.co.uk
134: Bieke Claessens/redcover.com
152: Ken Hayden/redcover.com
170: Lee Garland
www.leegarlandphotography.co.uk
192: Winfried Heinze/redcover.com
214: Ketchum/www.ketchum.com
020-7611-3500
232: Ken Hayden/redcover.com

All other illustrations and photographs are the
copyright of Quarto Inc. While every effort has
been made to credit the contributors, Quarto
would like to apologize should there have been
any omissions or errors—and would be pleased
to make the appropriate correction for future
editions of the book.

Color accuracy

Unfortunately for anyone who uses color, it is
always limiting when trying to reproduce real
color in a printed book, due to the limited
colors in printing inks. However, great length
and pain has gone into achieving good color
representation in this book, which can be
reproduced in your home, by you. The
positive outcome of this is that your final
interior will definitely be much more exciting
than the flat color on these pages!
It is important to remember that in printing
there may be very slight alterations in the
final color. Also, paint color may vary slightly
from one batch to another, so always try to
buy color made in the same batch.